SOUTH PARK

THE SCRIPTS: BOOK ONE

TREY PARKER
AND
MATT STONE

4 BOOKS

First published in the UK in 1999 by Channel 4 Books
an imprint of Macmillan Publishers Ltd
25 Eccleston Place London SW1W 9NF
Basingstoke and Oxford

www.macmillan.co.uk

Associated companies throughout the world

ISBN 07522 14675

9 8 7 6 5 4 3 2 1

A CIP catalogue record for this book is available from the British Library.

Designed by Blackjacks
Printed by New Interlitho, Spa, Milan.

CONTENTS

EPISODE 101

CARTMAN GETS AN ANAL PROBE

BY TREY PARKER & MATT STONE

CARTMAN GETS AN ANAL PROBE

EXT. SCHOOL BUS STOP - MORNING

STAN, KYLE AND KENNY wait in the snow for their school bus, holding their lunch boxes and debating.

KIDS
(Singing)
School days school days, teacher's golden -

Kyle's little brother, IKE, bounces into frame.

KYLE
- Ah damn it, my little brother's trying to follow me to school again.

IKE tries to talk.

IKE
BaBa Simi.

KYLE
Ike, you can't come to school with me!

IKE
BaBa Simi ba baa.

CARTMAN
Yeah, go home you little dildo.

KYLE
Dude! Don't call my brother a dildo.

STAN
What's a dildo?

KYLE
I don't know... and I'll bet Cartman doesn't know either!

CARTMAN
I know what it means!

KYLE
Well, what?!

CARTMAN
... I'm not telling you.

STAN
What's a dildo, Kenny?

Kenny talks, but we can't understand him through his thick coat.

KENNY
Mph rmph phrmph m phrmph mmr.

The boys all laugh.

CARTMAN
HA YEAH! THAT'S WHAT KYLE'S LITTLE BROTHER IS ALRIGHT!!

Suddenly, Kyle grabs Ike by the feet, swings him around, and bashes Cartman in the face.

CARTMAN (cont'd)
OW!

STAN
Dude that kicks ass!

KYLE
Yeah! Check this one out!
(to Ike)
Ready Ike? Kick the baby.

IKE
Don't kick the baby.

KYLE
Kick the baby.

Kyle kicks his brother down the icy road.

IKE
Wahhhhh!

Ike shoots down the road with a playful scream, and crashes head first into a group of mail boxes.

Cartman yawns grotesquely.

STAN
Whoa, Cartman, looks like you didn't get much sleep last night.

CARTMAN
That's 'cause I was having these bogus nightmares.

KYLE
Really, what about?

CARTMAN
Well, I dreamt that I was lying in my bed... In the dark...

INT. CARTMAN'S BEDROOM - DREAM SEQUENCE

Cartman is lying in his bed.

CARTMAN (V.O.)
... When all of a sudden this bright blue light filled the room.

A bright light fills the room.

CARTMAN (V.O.)
And slowly my bedroom door began to open...
And then the next thing I remember, I was being drug through a hallway!

INT. ALIEN SHIP - DREAM SEQUENCE

Cartman is being dragged by his ankles down a dark, organic corridor like the one seen in 'Fire In The Sky'.

CARTMAN (V.O.)
Then I was lying on a table, and these scary aliens wanted to operate on me! And they had big heads...
And big black eyes -

EXT. BUS STOP - (REALITY)

The boys are listening to Cartman's story with wide eyes and open mouths. Even little Ike is enthralled.

STAN
Dude! Visitors!

KYLE
Totally!

CARTMAN
What?

STAN
That wasn't a dream, Cartman, those were visitors!

CARTMAN
(Nervous)
No, it was just a dream. My mom said so!

STAN
Visitors are real!

KYLE
Yeah, they abduct people and they mutilate cows!

CARTMAN
Ah shut up, you guys, you're just trying to make me scared, and it's not working.

A large Chevy screeches to a halt. CHEF gets out of the car and approaches the kids.

CHEF
Hello there, children.

KIDS
Hey, Chef.

STAN
What's gonna be for lunch today, Chef?

CHEF
Well, today it's Salisbury steak with buttered noodles and a choice of green bean casserole or vegetable medley.

CARTMAN
Kick ass!

CHEF
Say, did any of you children see the alien spaceship last night?

CARTMAN
HUH?!

STAN
Yeah, fat boy saw it!

CARTMAN
No! Th-That was just a dream! And I'm NOT fat, I'm big-boned.

CHEF
(To Cartman)
Oh, was it the ones with the big long heads and the black eyes?

CARTMAN
(PETRIFIED)
AGH!

STAN
They took him on their ship!

CHEF
Ooh... Did they give you an anal probe?

CARTMAN
AGH!

STAN
What's an anal probe?

CHEF
That's when they put this big metal hoop-a-joo up your butt.

KYLE
Woa! They gave you an anal probe, Cartman?

CARTMAN
(Defensive)
No! I mean... Uh... Why would they do that?

STAN
Dude, they DID huh? Aliens stuck stuff up your ass!

CARTMAN
NO!

IKE
Ana Pobe!

CARTMAN
SHUT UP, DILDO!

CHEF
Well, I gotta get to the cafeteria. You children watch that fat boy now, he could be under alien control.

Chef turns to get back in his car and Cartman notices that the back of Chef's shirt has an EXACT image of the alien he saw, and the word 'Believe'.

CHEF peels off.

KYLE
We told you they were real Cartman.
Sorry to hear about your ass.

CARTMAN
(Extremely angry)
God Dammit, they didn't do anything to my ass!
It was just a dream!

The school bus pulls up and the boys start getting on.

KYLE
Why are you walking so funny, Cartman?

CARTMAN
Shut up!

Little Ike tries to follow his brother onto the bus.

IKE
I'll bla bblaa blaa.

KYLE
No, Ike! Go home!

Kyle gets ready to kick his brother.

IKE
Bla Wa Wah.

KYLE (cont'd)
This is it!! This one's for the game.

IKE
Bllaa aaahh haah.

KYLE
Kick the baby.

Kyle kicks his brother through the school bus window, and IKE flies into a snowbank.

The boys quickly get on the bus. Ike pulls his head out of the snow and looks around for his brother.

INT. SCHOOL BUS - MORNING

The kids walk past their mean old bus driver, MS. CRABTREE.

STAN
Good morning, Ms. Crabtree.

MS. CRABTREE
Sit down! We're running late!

Stan and Kyle walk to the back of the bus and take their seats. Cartman and Kenny sit up a few rows. Kyle looks out the back window to see Ike still standing at the bus stop.

KYLE
Dammit, he's still there!

STAN
Oh, don't worry about him.

KYLE
No, dude, if something happens to him my parents are gonna blame me!

MS. CRABTREE
SIT DOWN BACK THERE!! AAHHHH!!!

STAN
Yeah, whatever you fat bitch.

MS. CRABTREE
WHAT DID YOU SAY?!

STAN
I said I have a bad itch.

MS. CRABTREE
Oh.

Stan and Kyle sit down and the school bus moves on. Kyle turns around one last time to look at his brother.

KYLE
OH MY GOD!!!!

EXT. BUS STOP - DAY

A group of VISITORS, with large heads and almond-shaped eyes, surrounds Ike.

INT. - BUS

KYLE AND STAN
VISITORS!

Scared, Kenny pulls his hood shut.

KENNY
Mph mprmhpm bmarmphs!

KYLE
Ike!!!

EXT. BUS STOP - DAY

The visitors lead Ike to a large spacecraft hidden in the trees.

INT. BUS

KYLE
STOP THE BUS!

Kyle runs to the front of the bus.

KYLE (cont'd)
Ms. Crabtree, you have to stop this bus!

MS. CRABTREE
Do you want an office referral?!

KYLE
(SCARED)
No.

MS. CRABTREE
Then sit down!

KYLE
But I...

MS. CRABTREE
AAHH!!!

KYLE
AAHHH!!!!!

MS. CRABTREE & KYLE
AAHHHH!!!!!

Kyle runs to the back of the bus and hopelessly looks out the back window again just in time to see the spacecraft take off.

STAN
Cartman, are those the same visitors you saw?!

Cartman isn't looking.
He still thinks this is all a big joke.

CARTMAN
Shut up, you guys, it's not working.

KYLE
We have to do something!

STAN
Well, we can't do anything for now.
That fat bitch won't let us.

MS. CRABTREE
WHAT DID YOU SAY?!

STAN
I-I said that rabbits eat lettuce.

MS. CRABTREE
Oh...
(Pause)
Well, yes, they certainly do.

Ms. Crabtree turns the school bus violently and the children go flying everywhere screaming.

KYLE
What am I going to do?
My little brother's been abducted by aliens.

Stan farts.

KYLE (cont'd)
You farted!

The kids laugh.

CARTMAN
Somebody's baking brownies.

We see the alien spaceship leave the planet.

EXT. CATTLE RANCH - DAY

CATTLE RANCHER
That's the third cow this month, at this rate all my cattle are gonna die before the winter's through.

The cows look up with concern.

OFFICER BARBRADY
This is nothing out of the unusual.
Cows turn themselves inside out all the time.

The cows shake their heads.

CATTLE RANCHER
People been sayin' they've been seeing UFOs around.

OFFICER BARBRADY
UFOs?? Ha Ha.

CATTLE RANCHER
Yeah, and black army CIA helicopters and trucks.

OFFICER BARBRADY
That is the silliest thing I've ever heard.

Just then black army helicopters fly by.

CATTLE RANCHER
What was that?

OFFICER BARBRADY
That, that was a pigeon.

CATTLE RANCHER
What am I supposed to do, Barbrady? Just stand here and watch my cattle get mutilated one by one?

We see the aliens with grass in their hands whistling to the cows

CATTLE RANCHER (cont'd)
Hey, my cattle!! You see there is something funny going on.

OFFICER BARBRADY
There's nothing funny going on. I'll get those cows back.

INT. CLASSROOM - SOUTH PARK ELEMENTARY SCHOOL - DAY

MR. GARRISON
And now children, our friend Mr. Hat is going to tell us about Christopher Columbus.

Mr. Garrison has a ridiculous little puppet on his right hand that wears a striped hat.

MR. HAT
That's right Mr. Garrison. Christopher Columbus discovered America, and was the Indians' best friend. He helped the Indians win their war against Frederick Douglas, and... and freed the Hebrews from Napoleon, and discovered France.

KYLE
(TO STAN)
Oh man, I can't just sit here! I have to help my stupid brother or I'll come home without him and my dad will start yelling - 'Where's your brother, Kyle!' 'You weren't looking out for your little brother Kyle!'

STAN
Okay, okay, let's ditch school and go find him -

KYLE
'You know he can't think on his own, Kyle. Brush and floss, Kyle!' 'Where has that finger been, Kyle?!'

STAN
DUDE!

MR. GARRISON
Is there a problem, boys?

KYLE
Yes, Mr. Garrison, I have to go now.

MR. GARRISON
Oh really, Kyle? What is it this time? Another prostate tumor?

KYLE
No, my little brother has been abducted by aliens.

Mr. Garrison stares blankly at Kyle.

KYLE (cont'd)
It's true! Ask Cartman, they gave him an anal probe!

Cartman looks around at the other children, extremely embarrassed, and finally forces a little laugh as if to say it's all a little joke.

CARTMAN
Uhh... Huh, huh... That's a little joke.

Kyle steps to the front of class.

KYLE
Mr. Garrison, seriously, I HAVE to go! Can I PLEASE be excused from class?

MR. GARRISON
I don't know, Kyle. Did you ask Mr. Hat?

Kyle looks down at the stupid puppet on Garrison's hand.

KYLE
I don't want to ask Mr. Hat, I'm asking YOU!

MR. GARRISON
Oh, I think you should ask Mr. Hat.

KYLE
(SIGHING)
Mr. Hat, may I please be excused from class...?

Mr. Garrison shoves his puppeted hand violently in Kyle's face, and changes his voice.

MR. HAT
Well Kyle, NO! You hear me? You go to hell, you go to hell and you die!

MR. GARRISON
Hmm, guess you'll have to take your seat, Kyle.

KYLE
Dammit!

CARTMAN
Ha, ha! Mr. Hat yelled at you!

Just then, Cartman farts a HUGE fireball.

CARTMAN
AAAGHH!! Ow, my ass!

STAN
Damn, Cartman!

He farts another fireball.

CARTMAN
OW! OWWW MY ASS!!

KYLE
Dude, he's farting fire!

STAN
(pointing to Cartman)
It's the alien anal probe!
It's shooting fire from Cartman's rectum!!

CARTMAN
No, that was just a dream!

Cartman farts another flame.

MR. GARRISON
Eric, do you need to sit in the corner until your flaming gas is under control?

CARTMAN
No, Mr. Garrison. I'm fine.

Cartman farts a HUGE fireball which burns PIP, a little English boy.

PIP
OWWWW!!!!!

The class watches as their classmate runs out in flames.

ACT II

EXT. TRAIN CROSSING - DAY

A train is passing by and the cows are standing in line trying to get on.

TRAIN ENGINEER
Hey, you cows can't get on this train, this is a people train. You cows have no business on a people train, alright, 'cause you're cows.

The cows stare at the engineer.

TRAIN ENGINEER (cont'd)
No, no no, don't try any of that cow hypnosis on me alright, 'cause it's not going to work!!!

Just then, Officer Barbrady drives up with his sirens on.

OFFICER BARBRADY
Hold it right there cows.

Cows start to stampede away from Barbrady.

OFFICER BARBRADY (cont'd)
Come back here!

INT. SCHOOL CAFETERIA - DAY

The kids are all in line for lunch. Cartman farts a huge fireball.

CARTMAN
OOOOWWWW!!! Ooh, I sure am hungry.

STAN
How can you eat when you're farting fire?

CARTMAN
Shut up, dude. You're being totally immature.

KYLE
Hey look! There's Wendy Testaburger!

STAN
Where?

Adorable little WENDY TESTABURGER steps into the lunch line. ZOOM in on Stan who is absolutely in love. Little Hearts form all around his head - and Tchaikovsky's 'Romeo and Juliet' swells up.

The other boys see Stan's reaction and laugh.

CARTMAN (cont'd)
(Singing)
Stan wan-ts to ki-ss Wen-dy Testa-burger

STAN
Shut up Fat Ass! I don't even like her!

CARTMAN
I'm not fat - And you obviously like her, because you throw up every time she talks to you!

STAN
I do not!

Wendy walks up to the boys.

WENDY
Hi guys.

KYLE AND CARTMAN
Hi Wendy.

WENDY
Here Stan, this is for you.

Wendy hands Stan a note.

Stan VOMITS VIOLENTLY all over himself.

WENDY (cont'd)
Ew!

KYLE AND CARTMAN
Bye Wendy.

Wendy walks away.

KYLE
Dude, what does the note say?!

Stan opens the note and reads it.

STAN
Holy crap! it says she wants to meet ME at Starks Pond after school.

KYLE
Whoa, maybe you can kiss her.

CARTMAN
Or slip her the tongue.

KENNY
Mmmph mrrr mff Mrmmph

14
PAGE B
SHIFT
Scene
Panel
BG
Location/Time
Dialogue
KENNY
Mmmph mrrr mff Mrmmph
Action/Efx
Trans.
SOUTH PARK
15
Scene
Panel
BG
Location/Time
Dialogue
STAN
"What? How do you know she has a cat?"
Action/Efx
Trans.
16
PAGE 6
Scene
Panel
BG
SCHOOL FOOD IS GOOD FOOD
Location/Time
Dialogue
Action/Efx
After a painfully long pause,
Trans.

16
Scene
Panel
BG
School FOOD IS GOOD FOOD
Location/Time

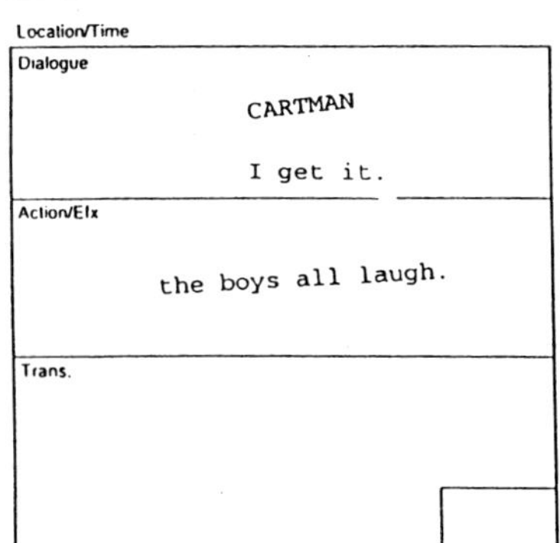
Dialogue
CARTMAN
I get it.
Action/Efx
the boys all laugh.
Trans.

SOUTH PARK
17
Scene
Panel
BG
Location/Time

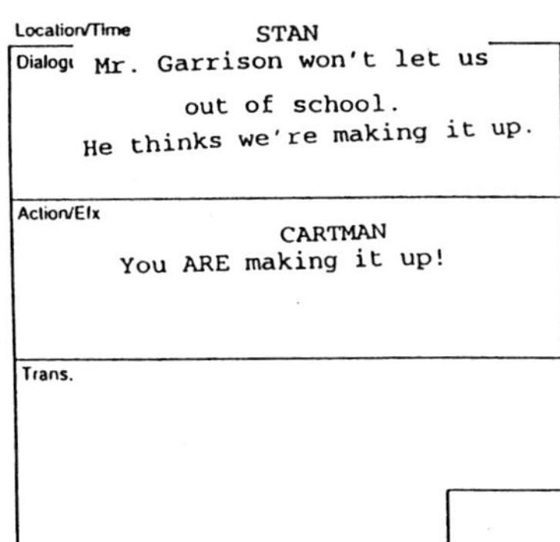
STAN
Dialogue
Mr. Garrison won't let us
out of school.
He thinks we're making it up.
Action/Efx
CARTMAN
You ARE making it up!
Trans.

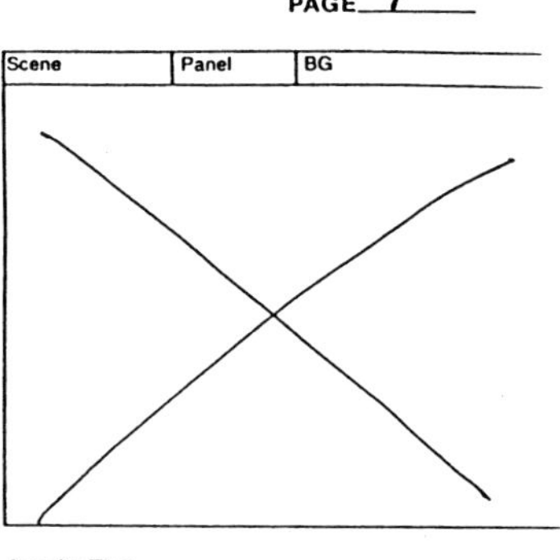
PAGE 7
Scene
Panel
BG
Location/Time
Dialogue
Action/Efx
Trans.

STAN
What? How do you know she has a cat?

After a painfully long pause, the boys all laugh.

CARTMAN
I get it.

KYLE
C'mon you guys, we need to figure out how to get out of school so we can get my little brother back!

The boys make it to the front of the line, where Chef is handing lunch trays to the boys and girls.

CHEF
Hello there children.

KIDS
Hey, Chef.

CHEF
How are you doing?

KYLE
Bad.

CHEF
Why bad?

KYLE
Chef, have you ever had something happen to you... But nobody believed you?

CHEF
Aw, children, children, that's a problem we've ALL had to face at some time or another. Here, let me sing you a little song... It might clear things up.

Music swells up.

CHEF (cont'd)
(SINGING)
I'm gonna make love to you woman, gonna lay you down by the fire - And caress your womanly body, make you moan and perspire -

STAN
Ah Chef, Chef.

CHEF
- Gonna get those juices flowin' -

STAN
Chef!

CHEF
- We're making love gravy, love gravy -

STAN
Chef!!!!!

CHEF
- Love, love, love... GRAVY!!! -

STAN
CHEF!!

The music stops.

CHEF
Huh, do you feel better?

KYLE
No!

CHEF
Oh, come on children, what can be so bad?
It's Salisbury steak day!

STAN
Visitors took Kyle's baby brother.

CHEF
WHAT?!

Chef runs around the counter and
kneels down by the kids.

CHEF (cont'd)
(Whispering)
Well what the hell are you doing in school, eating
Salisbury steak?! Go find him, dammit!

STAN
Mr. Garrison won't let us out of school.
He thinks we're making it up.

CARTMAN
You ARE making it up!

Just then, Cartman farts another fireball.
But this time, a long, metal object emerges from his ass.
It opens like a robotic eye and looks around.

STAN
Woa!

CARTMAN
What?

The eye looks around, blinks, then closes itself and zips back into Cartman's ass.

KYLE
That was cool!

Chef spins Cartman around and looks at his ass.

CHEF
It's some kind of sembiodic metamorphosis device. This could mean the visitors want to communicate with us!

CARTMAN
Oh, I see, now YOU'RE going to join in on the little joke, huh?

CHEF
It's no joke children, this is big!

KYLE
(pleading)
Please Chef, if I don't get out of school and get my little brother back from the aliens, my parents are gonna disown me.

Chef thinks for a second.

CHEF
Ah, hold on now... You got to help the children!

CARTMAN
You guys sure are going a long way to try to scare me. I WANT MY SALISBURY STEAK!!!

Chef pulls the fire alarm.

CHEF
Fire Drill!!! Fire Drill, everybody out. Okay children, this is your chance.

The boys all take off.

STAN
Killer, thanks Chef.

CHEF
Man oh man, first contact with the alien visitors. I've got to get myself ready...

EXT. LITTLE TOWN - SOUTH PARK

Kids are singing.

KIDS
We got out of school... No more school today...
We got out of school.

Cartman farts a fireball.

CARTMAN
OHHHH - YOU GUYS, MY ASS!! SERIOUSLY!

STAN
Okay, Cartman, you can stop farting fire now.

CARTMAN
I would if I could you son of a bitch!

KYLE
Okay, so how do we get my little brother back?

CARTMAN
Would you stop going on about your little brother?! I KNOW it was just a dream! I KNOW I didn't have an anal probe! And I KNOW that I'm not under alien control!!!

Suddenly, there is a loud BZAP!!!
Cartman's expression completely changes.

His eyes widen - and his mouth curls into a false smile. Strange '30s music starts to play from nowhere and Cartman starts to sing (although his voice isn't his own).

CARTMAN (cont'd)
(Singing)
I love to sing-a! About the moon-a and the June-a and the spring-a! I love to sing-a!

Stan and Kyle look on, perplexed.

CARTMAN (cont'd)
About a sky of blue or a tea for two.

Just as suddenly as it started, the music stops and Cartman goes back to his normal self. The boys all stare at each other. Cartman looks absolutely baffled.

STAN
What the hell was that?!

KYLE
He is under alien control.
That thing in his butt is linked up to the visitors.

CARTMAN
Oh, son of a bitch.

ACT III FADE OUT.

FADE IN:

CARTMAN
You guys shut up, I'm not under alien control.

Kyle walks up to Cartman's ear and starts screaming in it.

KYLE (cont'd)
HEY!! IF YOU VISITORS CAN HEAR ME - BRING ME BACK MY LITTLE BROTHER GOD DAMMIT!

CARTMAN
Ow! That hurts, you butt licker!

Suddenly, a small alien scout ship flies by.

STAN
KYLE, LOOK! It's them!

Kyle picks a rock up off the ground.

KYLE
GIVE ME BACK MY BROTHER!

Kyle throws the rock at the UFO. DING! The UFO stops and fires a yellow ray at the boys. The ray hits Kenny, and blows him back several yards. Kenny lands with a horrible bone-breaking CRUNCH!

STAN
Oh my God!! They killed Kenny!

KYLE
YOU BASTARDS!! COME BACK HERE!! COME BAAAAACK!

But the little UFOs disappears into the sky.

KYLE (cont'd)
DAMMIT! We were so close!

STAN
Hey, look - I think Kenny's okay!

Kenny manages to pick himself up off the ground. He looks pretty bad, but he might be -

Just then the cows come stampeding through and run over Kenny.

KENNY
Mff mrrr mph.

VWOOM!! Officer Barbrady's car races through frame and runs over Kenny.

The boys walk over to Kenny's bleeding body.

STAN
Wow, poor Kenny.

KYLE
Now do you believe us Cartman?

CARTMAN
No!

STAN
Cartman, they KILLED Kenny!

CARTMAN
He's not dead.

STAN
Dude, Kenny is dead! See?!

CARTMAN
Shut up, you guys.

KYLE
(Pulling Kenny's head off)
He's DEAD, Cartman.

CARTMAN
GOD DAMMIT I DIDN'T HAVE AN ANAL PROBE!!!

There is a long pause.

CARTMAN (cont'd)
Screw you guys, I'm going home!

Cartman walks away.

KYLE
Go on and go home you Fat Chicken!

CARTMAN
(O.S.)
Dildo!

KYLE
You're all I have left, Stan.

STAN
Sorry dude, I gotta go meet Wendy Testaburger.

KYLE
You can't! Poor Ike must be so scared...
Up there all alone... You gotta help me, dude!

STAN
Dude, like Chef says, I gotta get a piece of loving while the gettin's hot.

Stan walks away.

Rats come into frame and feast on Kenny's dead body.

KYLE (cont'd)
Rats!

INT. CARTMAN'S HOUSE - DUSK

Cartman walks into his house and is greeted by his overly pleasant MOTHER.

MRS. CARTMAN
Hello Eric.

CARTMAN
Hi Mom.

MRS. CARTMAN
How are you doing?

CARTMAN
Well, I'm pissed off.

MRS. CARTMAN
Here, I made you powder doughnut pancake surprise.

CARTMAN
I don't want powder doughnut pancake surprise! All the kids at school call me fat!

MRS. CARTMAN
You're not fat, you're big-boned.

CARTMAN
That's what I said.

MRS. CARTMAN
You can have an eency weency bit can't you?

CARTMAN
NO!

MRS. CARTMAN
Just a weency eency woo woo.

CARTMAN
NO! Leave me alone Mom!

MRS. CARTMAN
How about a nice chocolate chicken pot-pie, then?

CARTMAN
What? Well, that does sound pretty good.

Cartman sits down at the couch and turns on the T.V.

CARTMAN (cont'd)
Uh, Mom?

MRS. CARTMAN
Yes, hon?

CARTMAN
If anybody calls or comes over - I'm not here, okay?

MRS. CARTMAN
Sure, hon. You want some Cheesy Poofs too?

CARTMAN
Yeah I want Cheesy Poofs!

EXT. STARK'S POND - AFTERNOON

Stan and Kyle are standing at Stark's pond.

KYLE
Well, looks like she's not gonna show up, Stan.
Let's go look for the visitors now.

STAN
But her note said she'd be here!

WENDY
Hi Stan.

Wendy appears from frame left.
Stan immediately vomits all over himself.

WENDY
Ew!

KYLE
You can't talk to Stan, Wendy, he throws up when you do.

WENDY
But why, Stan?

Stan vomits some more.

WENDY
Ew!

KYLE
Look, could you guys just get down to business so we can
go find my little brother?

WENDY
Huh?

KYLE
Just make sweet love down by the fire.

WENDY
What happened to your little brother?

INT. CARTMAN'S HOUSE - LATE AFTERNOON

Cartman is still busy eating and watching T.V.

ANGLE - TELEVISION

A T.V. REPORTER stands out in a random wheat field.

T.V. REPORTER
As the reports of UFO sightings increase, more mysterious crop-circle patterns are appearing in fields all around South Park. These crop-circles, when viewed from above, form strange patterns...

ZOOM OUT to show a huge crop-circle that looks EXACTLY like Cartman.

RESUME - CARTMAN ON COUCH

CARTMAN
Hey, that kinda looks like... Tom Selleck.

T.V. REPORTER (O.S.)
Could it be that aliens are trying to make contact with us here on Earth?

Just then, Cartman's cute little kitty, KITTY, walks up and looks at him innocently. The kitty meows.

CARTMAN
No Kitty... This is MY pot-pie.

The cat meows again.

CARTMAN (cont'd)
No Kitty! Bad Kitty!! No Kitty, this is MY pot-pie!!! MOMM!!! Kitty's being a dildo!!

Cartman's mother appears from the kitchen.

CARTMAN'S MOM
Well then I know a certain kitty kitty who's sleeping with mommy tonight.

CARTMAN
What?

EXT. STARK'S POND - AFTERNOON

Kyle is finishing his story to Wendy.

KYLE
... And now I have to go home without him and my parents are going to have me killed!

WENDY
Well, why don't you go get the fat kid?

KYLE
Why?

WENDY
Well if the fat kid has something implanted in his ass, maybe the visitors are using him as part of their plan. You should use the fat kid as bait to bring them back.

KYLE
Hey, you're right Wendy! C'mon Stan, We have to go get Cartman!

WENDY
C'mon Stan!

Stan vomits.

WENDY
Ewwww!

STAN
Hey wait, when do I get to make sweet love?

INT. CARTMAN'S HOUSE - AFTERNOON

CARTMAN
No Kitty!! You can't have any!!

The cat puts its paw up and meows cutely.

CARTMAN (cont'd)
NO KITTY! THIS IS MY POT-PIE! BAD KITTY!!

Cartman farts a fireball onto his cat. The cat runs away, on fire, making horrible sounds.

CARTMAN (cont'd)
Oh, excuse me, Kitty.

Cartman's mother opens the door to reveal Stan, Kyle and Wendy.

MRS. CARTMAN
Eric, look who's here!

CARTMAN
Dude, WEAK mom!

KYLE
Come on, Eric, we're going to go play at the bus stop.

CARTMAN
I can't - My mom says -

MRS. CARTMAN
That's okay, Eric. I think you need to spend time with your little friends.

CARTMAN
But mom, I don't want to spend time with my little friends.

MRS. CARTMAN
Don't be difficult, Eric.
Now you go out and play in the fun snow.

CARTMAN
God dammit!

The burning kitty races through frame.

EXT. REMOTE LOCATION BY A TREE - NIGHT

Stan ties a rope to Cartman's ankle.
Kyle ties the other end to a nearby tree.

CARTMAN
(EXTREMELY NERVOUS)
You guys, I have to get home.

STAN
Don't be such a fraidy cat, Cartman! This rope will make sure they can't take you on board again.

Wendy, Stan and Kyle walk over to some bushes and crouch down, leaving Cartman all alone in the darkness.

Cartman stares up nervously at the starry, ominous sky.

CARTMAN
Oh man, this sucks.

KYLE
How come the visitors aren't coming for him?

STAN
I think we need to signal them somehow.

Cartman farts and a flame lights up the surroundings.

PROD. #
SC.
35
SOUTH PARK
36
37
A
PAGE 15
Scene
Panel
BG
Location/Time
Dialogue
CARTMAN
I'm sick of it! It's completely immature!!!
Action/Efx
Reverse Cartman
Trans.
(after 'ok. that does it.)
STAN
Hey! It's happening again!
This time, the rod looks around, then expands, and expands, folds over onto itself and expands again, until finally an eighty foot satellite dish is sticking out of Cartman's ass.
37
SOUTH PARK
37
SOUTH PARK
38
16
KYLE
Woa! Look at that!
STAN
Now do you believe us Cartman?!

CARTMAN
OWWWWW!

WENDY
Hey, he's like Rudolph!

KYLE
Yeah, all you have to do is fart some more, Cartman, and the visitors are sure to come.

CARTMAN
Really? Uhh... I don't think I have to fart anymore tonight.

KYLE
Sure you do!

STAN
Come on, Cartman! Fart!

CARTMAN
I don't wanna...

STAN
He can't hold it in forever.

KYLE
Fart, damn you!

CARTMAN
Okay!! That does it!!! Now listen! Why is it that everything today has involved things either going in or coming out of MY ASS?! I'm sick of it! It's completely immature!!!

Suddenly, the metal rod emerges once again from Cartman's ass.

STAN
Hey! It's happening again!

This time, the rod looks around, then expands, and expands, folds over onto itself and expands again, until finally an eighty-foot satellite dish is sticking out of Cartman's ass.

KYLE
Woa! Look at that!

STAN
Now do you believe us Cartman?!

Cartman glances quickly at the dish.

39

PAGE

Scene | Panel | BG

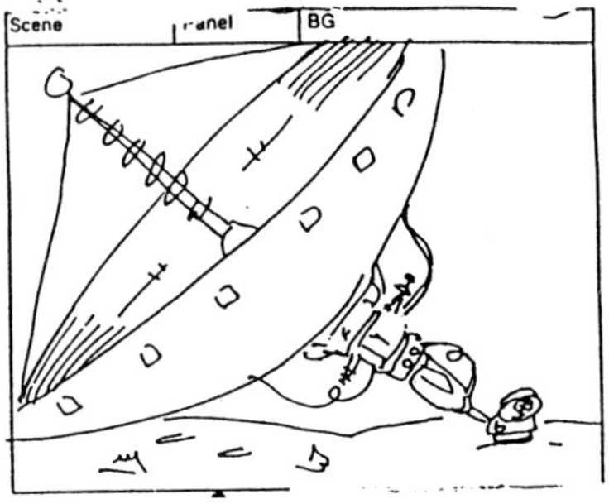

Location/Time

Dialogue

CARTMAN

You guys can't scare me! I know you're making it all up!

Trans.

CARTMAN

Sure, guys, whatever.

PROD #

SC.

40

Scene | Panel | BG

Location/Time

Dialogue

STAN

Cartman! There's an eighty foot satellite dish sticking out of your ass!

41

PAGE 17

41

Scene | Panel | BG

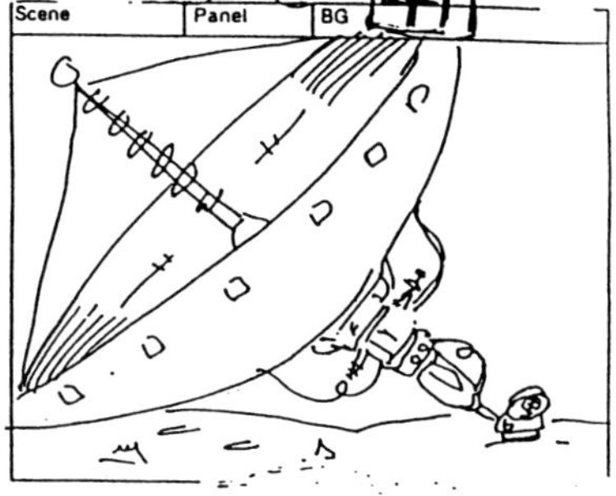

Dialogue

CARTMAN

Sure, guys, whatever.

Action/Efx

41

The dish powers up with a low hum and a huge yellow beam of light shoots out from it like a searchlight.

PROD. #

SC.

42

Scene | Panel | BG

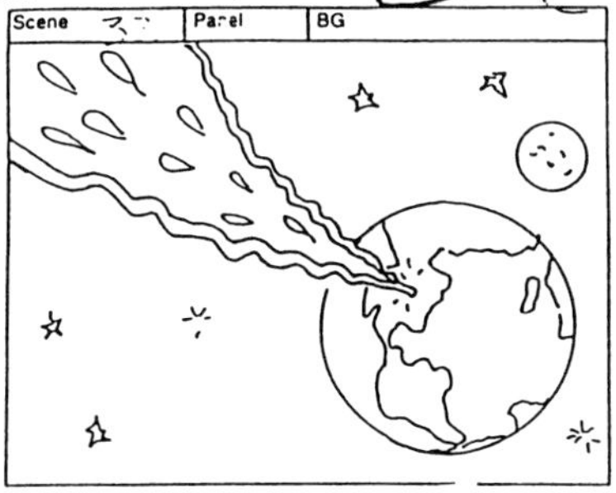

Location/Time EXT. OUTER SPACE

Dialogue

Action/Efx

beam of light emulates from Earth and shoots outwards into space.

SOUTH PARK

SC.

Loc

Dialogue

Action/Efx

Trans.

43 44

PAGE 18

SC.

Scene | Panel | BG

Location/Time EXT. CHEF'S BACK YARD

Dialogue

CHEF

Oh, boy! The aliens are going to make first contact! What a glorious day for mankind!

Action/Efx

CHEF

(Shouting)

Hey, down here, aliens! We are ready for your wisdom!

Trans.

Chef swigs a beer.

CARTMAN
You guys can't scare me! I know you're making it all up!

STAN
Cartman! There's an eighty-foot satellite dish sticking out of your ass!

CARTMAN
Sure you guys, whatever.

The dish powers up with a low hum and a huge yellow beam of light shoots out from it like a searchlight.

EXT. OUTER SPACE

The beam of light emulates from Earth and shoots outwards into space.

EXT. CHEF'S BACK YARD

Chef is dressed in party clothes and sunglasses. He is sitting in a lounge chair out on his front lawn. He has a little sign that reads 'Welcome Visitors!'

Chef notices the big bright light.

CHEF
Oh, boy! The aliens are going to make first contact!

Chef swigs a beer.

CHEF
(Shouting)
Hey, down here! We are ready for your wisdom!
(Checking his watch)
And you only got twenty minutes before 'Sanford and Son' is on!

RESUME - FIELD

CARTMAN
YOU GUYS! I AM SERIOUSLY GETTING PISSED OFF RIGHT NOW! I KNOW THERE'S NO SUCH THING AS ALIENS!!

Just then, a **HUGE** alien mother ship drops down from the sky directly above Cartman. It is quickly followed by several scout ships.

CARTMAN
OH, GOD DAMMIT!!

Mr. Garrison is driving by and stops when he sees all the commotion.

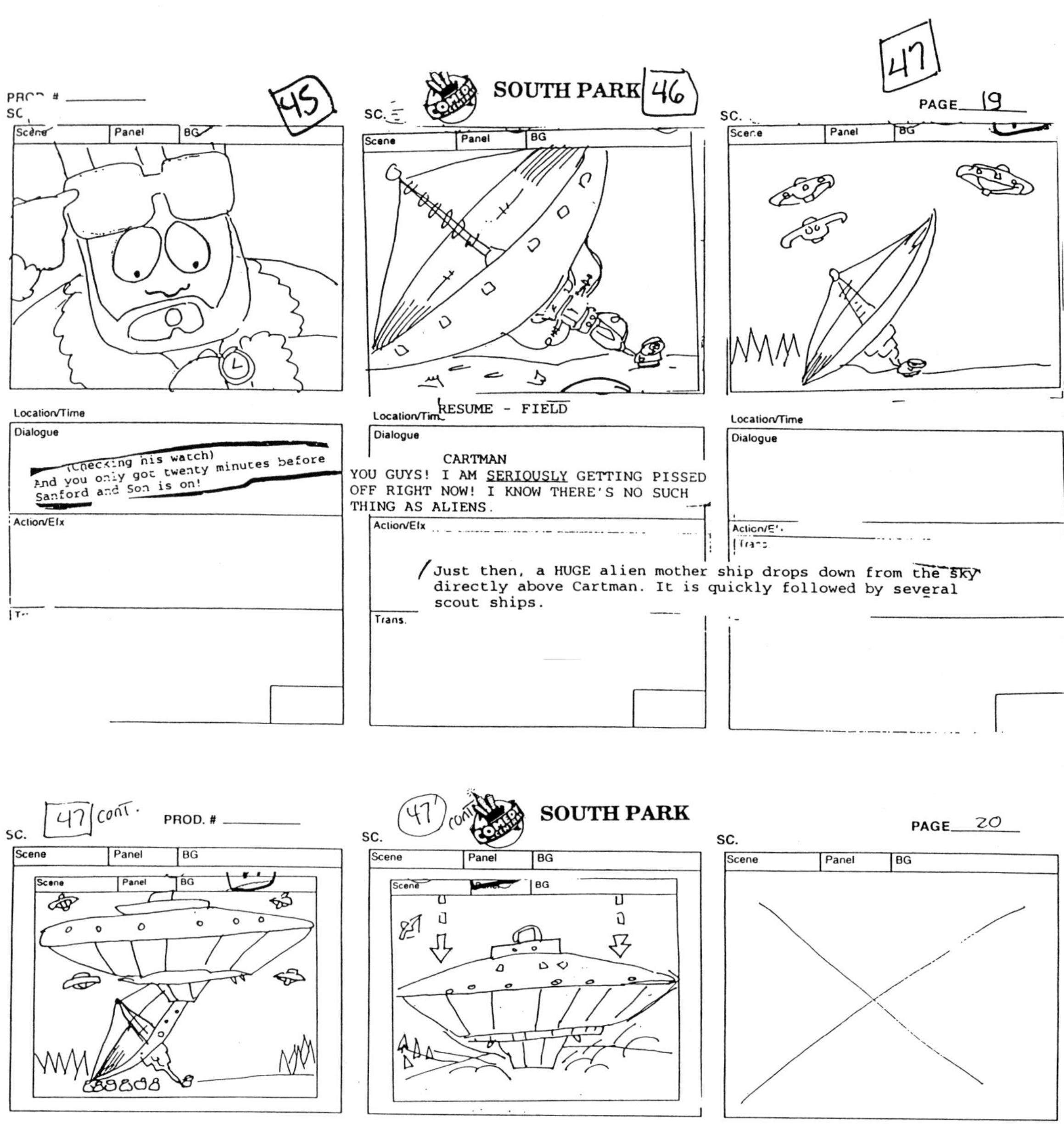

Location/Time

Dialogue

CARTMAN
OH, GOD DAMMIT!!

Action/Efx

Trans.

Location/Time

Dialogue

Action/Efx

Trans.

Location/Time

Dialogue

Action/Efx

Trans.

MR. GARRISON
What the? I tell you, there is some crazy stuff going on in this town.

Mr. Hat pops up.

MR. HAT
You can say that again, Mr. Garrison.

KYLE
Come down here you stinkin' aliens!

Five aliens beam down, and instantly appear in front of Stan, Kyle, and Wendy. The kids are really scared.

STAN
Go on, Kyle, ask them for your little brother back...

KYLE
(Tenderly)
V-Visitors... This morning you took my brother, Ike. He's the little freckled kid that looks like a football...

The Visitors stare at Kyle.

KYLE (cont'd)
At first I was happy you took him away... But I've learned something today; that having a little brother is a pretty special thing.

STAN
Yeah...

Violin music swells up.

KYLE
Aw, heck, Mr. Visitors, I'm just a kid all alone in this crazy world, but if you could just find it in your hearts or whatever you have to give my brother back to me, it sure would make my life brighter again

Kyle bows his head down and starts to sob.

STAN
That was beautiful, dude.

KYLE
(still looking down)
Did it work?

STAN
Nope, they're leaving.

KYLE
HEY YOU SCRAWNY ASS (BEEP)-HEADS!

The visitors turn around.

KYLE (cont'd)
WHAT'S THE (BEEP) IS WRONG WITH YOU, YOU (BEEP) LITTLE (BEEP). YOU MUST BE SOME KIND OF (BEEP) TO BE ABLE TO IGNORE A CRYING CHILD.

Stan is absolutely shocked.

STAN
Woa, dude.

KYLE
YOU KNOW WHAT YOU LIKE!? I BET YOU'D ALL LIKE TO (BEEP) YOUR OWN (BEEP) WHILE SHE (BEEP) ON YOUR (BEEP) (BEEP)!!

STAN
Hey Wendy, what's a (BEEEEEP)

Wendy shrugs.

Suddenly, a large door on the alien mothership opens. Ike is entombed in some sort of alien machinery. He is being spun around and is shocked with all sorts of alien electricity but generally looks as happy as he always does.

IKE
Blaa Ba Wah Wahh.

KYLE
Ike! Jump down now for the love of God Ike, JUMP!!!!

IKE
Bo ham me!

Just then, the herd of cows comes running in The cows come to a screeching halt RIGHT IN FRONT of the aliens! Their poor little cow eyes grow wide and they start to shake.

The visitors stare at the cows. The cows shiver, they have nowhere to run. Finally, one of the visitors raises its hand in a Vulcan-like gesture.

VISITOR
Moo.

The cows all look suprised.

VISITOR
Mooo. Moooo. Mooo.
SUBTITLES: Greetings, cows of Earth. We come in peace.

The cows all look at each other. Finally, one cow makes a noise.

COW
Moo?
SUBTITLES: Really?

Meanwhile, Kyle and the kids are still trying to get Ike to jump down.

KYLE
Come on, Ike! I promise I'll be nice to you from now on!

IKE
Don kick da bebe!

The visitors continue to moo at the cows.

VISITOR
Moo. Moo. Moo.
SUBTITLES: We have experimented with all the beings of Earth, and have learned that you are the most intelligent and wise.

CARTMAN
What the hell are they talking about?!

COW
Moo. Moo, moo?
SUBTITLES: Why did you turn some of us inside out?

The visitors look at each other.

VISITOR
Moo, moo, moo. Moo.
SUBTITLES: Oh, that was Carl's fault. He's new.

Another visitor steps forward and raises his hand in the background.

VISITOR CARL
Moo. Moo.
SUBTITLES: Yeah, sorry about that. My bad.

KYLE
Ike!!!!!

The visitors hand over a small clear obelisk and place it on the ground in front of the cows, who just stare at it.

VISITOR
Moo, moo, moo. Moo.
SUBTITLES: Take this device. It is a gift from us.

Kyle stands underneath his brother, who still won't jump down.

KYLE
Ike! Do your impersonation of David Caruso's career.

IKE
It's my tun!

Finally, Ike jumps from the machine and lands upside down in the snow. The large satellite dish collapses and disappears back into Cartman's ass.

VISITOR
Moo, moo, moo. Moo.
SUBTITLES: Farewell, cows, peace be with you.

The visitors disappear and beam up to their ship. A light shines down on Cartman and sucks him up.

CARTMAN
You guys! Get me down from here!!

Flames shoot out of Cartman's ass in a flaming fart. The flames burn the rope and Cartman goes shooting upwards.

CARTMAN FLOATS UP INTO THE SPACECRAFT.
ONCE INSIDE, THE HATCH CLOSES AND THE SHIP TAKES OFF.
IN THE DISTANCE, THE KIDS CAN HEAR CARTMAN.

CARTMAN
Heeeeeeelp..... Sons a bitcheeees!! DIIIIILLLLLDOOOS!!

With the UFO gone, the forest is silent once again.

STAN
I'm sure glad that's over with.

KYLE
Yeah, boy am I glad to see you, Ike!

IKE
Oh he fly at the sky.

EXT. CHEF'S BACK YARD

CHEF
Wait, where are you going, alien visitors? Come back!!!

LADY #1
Well chef, where's this amazing thing you're going to show us?

CHEF
Well, it's in the bedroom, ladies, come on in.

CUT TO:

KYLE
C'mon Ike, we can make it just in time for dinner.

Kyle and Ike walk away, leaving Stan and Wendy alone.

STAN
Thanks for your help, Wendy.

WENDY
Whatever, dude.

STAN
Hey, I didn't throw up!

WENDY
Cool!

Stan and Wendy move closer as if about to kiss... closer... closer... And finally - Stan vomits all over himself and Wendy.

WENDY (cont'd)
Ew!

STAN
Sorry.

WENDY
Hey look! A French fry!

STAN
Cool!

WENDY
And what is that?

STAN
I think it's part of a Cheesy Poof.

WENDY
Hey, what's that?

Wendy and Stan continue to identify foodstuffs in Stan's vomit, silhouetted against a full moon.

FADE OUT.

EXT. BUS STOP - MORNING

Stan and Kyle wait for the bus.

STAN
Gee, the bus'll be here any minute and Cartman still isn't around.

KYLE
Yeah, we're running out of friends.

STAN
I wonder what that thing was the visitors gave the cows?

The cows graze peacefully.
They have their little object with them.

Officer Barbrady walks in.

OFFICER BARBRADY
Ha ha cows, I got you cornered.
Let's see you get away now!

One of the cows steps on the object that the aliens gave them and a ray shoots out and hits Officer Barbrady who begins to dance and sing (although his voice isn't his own) the way Cartman did when he was under the alien control.

OFFICER BARBRADY (cont'd)
(Singing)
I love to sing-a! About the moon-a and the June-a and the spring-a! I love to sing-a! About a sky of blue or a tea for two.

The cows jump up and down gleefully.

RESUME - BOYS AT BUS STOP

SUDDENLY, CARTMAN DROPS FROM THE SKY AND LANDS WITH A DULL THUD INTO THE SNOW.

STAN
Oh, hey Cartman!

Cartman moans. The school bus pulls up.

KYLE
Wow, Cartman, the visitors dropped you off just in time to go to school!

CARTMAN
Oh man, I had this crazy nightmare last night...

STAN
Really? What about?

CARTMAN
Well, I was standing out in a field and I had this **HUGE** satellite dish stickin' outta my butt. And then there was hundreds of cows and aliens, and then I went up on the ship and Scott Baio gave me pink eye.

STAN
That wasn't a dream Cartman. That really happened!

CARTMAN
Oh right, why don't I have pink eye then?

KYLE
Cartman, you DO have pink eye!

Sure enough, Cartman's eyes are a bright shade of pink.

CARTMAN
Ah, son of a bitch.

FIN

EPISODE 104

BIG GAY AL'S BIG GAY BOAT RIDE

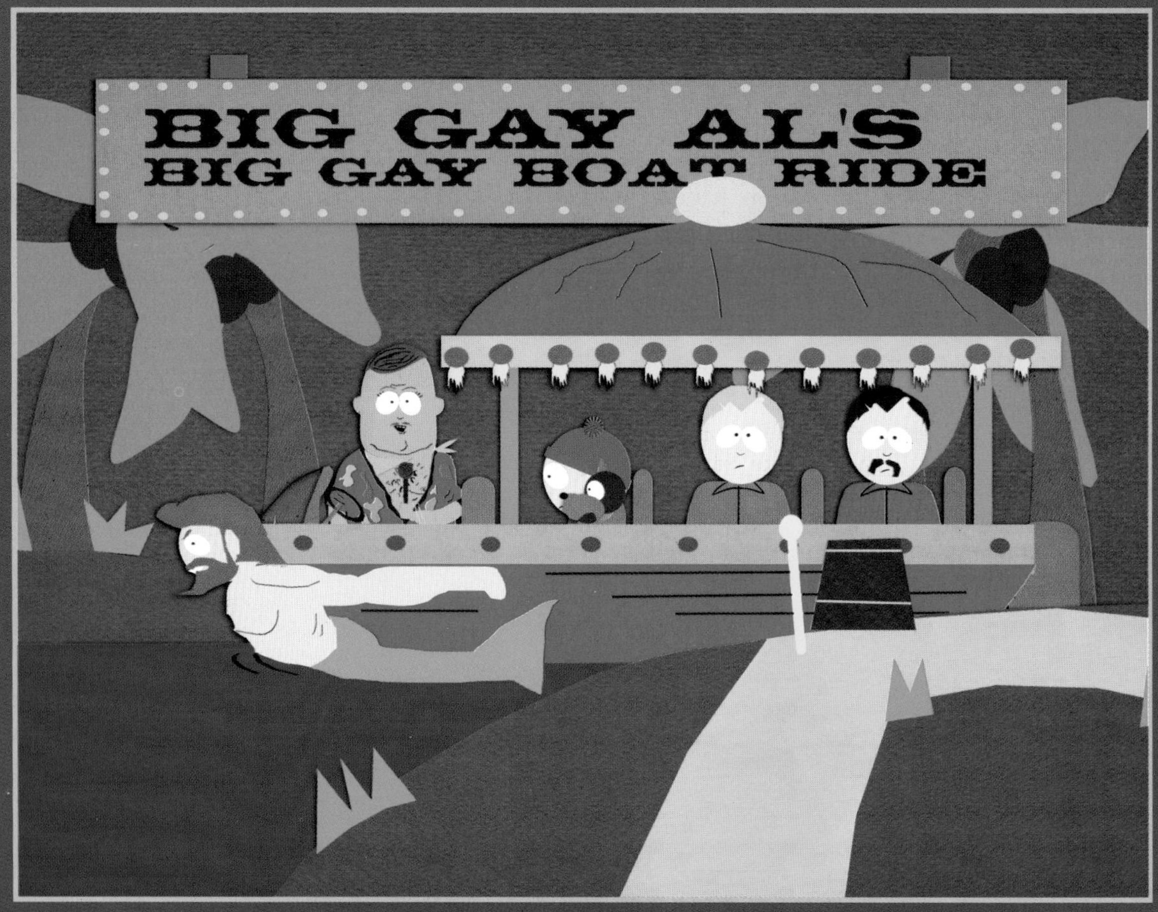

BY TREY PARKER & MATT STONE

EXT. BUS STOP - DAY

The boys are waiting for their bus.

KYLE
Hey, where's the school bus?
We're gonna be late for football practice.

A dog comes walking up to Stan wagging its tail.

STAN
Hiya Sparky!

KYLE
Who's that?

STAN
That's my new dog, Sparky.
(Proudly) He followed me to the bus stop!

KYLE
Wow, cool!

STAN
Good boy, Sparky! Who's my best buddy?
Who's your boy? Who's your buddy?

CARTMAN
Ugh, you're making me sick, dude.

STAN
He's part Dobermann, and part wolf!
He's the toughest dog on the mountain!

CARTMAN
No way. Everybody knows that Sylvester is
the toughest dog in South Park!

WHIP PAN to a mangy mutt bulldog sitting on the curb
that looks ridiculously fierce and pissed off.

STAN
He's not meaner than Sparky!

CARTMAN
Oh yeah? Let's see... HEY SYLVESTER!

Sylvester angrily walks over to the boys.
He and Sparky immediately growl at each other.

STAN
Sparky'll kick his ass!

CARTMAN
I'll put a dollar on Sylvester!

KYLE
You're on, dude!

Sparky and the other dog circle each other.
Finally Sparky lunges!

STAN
That's it, Sparky, kick his ass!

Sparky hops on top of the other dog. We see only the top part of Sparky and the boys' faces, which all look confused.

CARTMAN
Huh... He's doing something to his ass.
He's not kicking his ass, but he's definitely doing something to his ass.

STAN
Sparky?! Bad dog.

KENNY
Mphph rmph rm rmph!

STAN
WHAT?

CARTMAN
Yeah dude, I think your dog is gay!

STAN
What do you mean?

CARTMAN
That dog is a gay homosexual.

STAN
(To the boys)
He's just confused.

KYLE
I think the OTHER dog's the one that's confused.

KENNY
Mph rmph rmph!

STAN
Sick, shut up, dude!

Finally, Sylvester runs away yelping.

CARTMAN
(Singing)
Stan's dog's a homo! Stan's dog's a homo!

Cartman is cut off by the big yellow bus entering frame.

EXT. FOOTBALL FIELD - DAY

The large football field sits behind South Park Elementary. The boys are all dressed in cute little football uniforms, with 'South Park Cows' on the jerseys and a cow's head on the helmet.

CHEF
Okay children, I know that you're all extremely excited, nervous and anxious about the homecoming game against Middle Park -

KYLE
Who's Middle Park?

CARTMAN
What's homecoming?

CHEF
- But just remember what I taught you: that football is like making love to a really beautiful woman; you can't always score, but when you do it makes all the trying worth while.

The kids blink.

CHEF
Now let's start practice!

Chef blows his whistle and the kids put on their helmets and walk to the field.

PIP
Ah, Mr. Chef, sir?

CHEF
Yes, Pip, what is it?

PIP
Well I still don't have a helmet.

CHEF
I know, Pip, the school can't afford helmets for everybody.

PIP
Yes, but, couldn't we ROTATE who doesn't have a helmet every week? Does it always have to be me?

CHEF
Yes, Pip, I'm afraid it does.

PIP
Oh.

CHEF
Sorry, son, now get your ass in there.

Pip joins the other kids, who are in huddled positions at the line of scrimmage. Stan plays quarterback.

STAN
HUT! HUT! HUT! HUT! HUT! HUT! HUT! HUT! HUT! HUT! HUT! HUT!

CHEF
HIKE THE DAMN BALL!!

Cartman snaps the ball, which goes flying past Stan. The kids all yell and run around in circles. Kyle charges Pip head first, smashing Pip's helmetless head open. Chef rolls his eyes as Jimbo and Ned come walking up.

JIMBO
Hey, how's practice coming there, Chef?

CHEF
Huh? Oh, fine, fine.

JIMBO
I don't have to remind you just how important this game is to us South Park alumni.

CHEF
Elementary school alumni?

JIMBO
That's as far as most of us got. You think we have a shot at beating the spread against Middle Park this year?

CHEF
I don't know? What's the spread?

JIMBO
Middle Park by seventy points.

CHEF
Hmmm...

Chef looks over at the kids who are running around in circles. Cartman takes the ball and immediately falls over on top of Kenny.

CHEF
I don't think we have a chance.

JIMBO
Nonsense, not with MY nephew at quarterback! Right, Stanley?!

STAN
Huh?

Stan turns and gets smacked in the head with the football. He falls down, but then quickly gets up, grabs the ball and throws an incredible long bomb... At the other end, Kyle catches the ball!

JIMBO
Atta boy!!

CHEF
Great pass, Stan!

JIMBO
C'mon, Ned, we gotta get our asses to the bookie!

Jimbo and Ned dash off.

EXT. NEAR FOOTBALL FIELD - DAY

The boys are all taking off their uniforms.

CHEF
Okay, that was a good practice children, we'll see you here again tomorrow.

KYLE
Hey Stan, isn't that your dog?

Stan looks to see that Sparky is prancing onto the playing field.

STAN
Yeah, he must have followed me to football practice. You see? He IS smart!

KID (CLYDE)
Aw, my dog Rex follows me to football practice all the time.

Little Rex just sits there. Sparky walks over to it.

STAN
Yeah, but MY dog found his own way here! That makes him smarter than your - SPARKY get down!!

KID (CLYDE)
OH MY GOD, WHAT IS HE DOING TO MY DOG?!?!

CARTMAN
There he goes again!

STAN
GET DOWN SPARKY! DOWN!

CARTMAN
Stan forgot to mention that his dog is a gay homosexual.

KID (CLYDE)
Make him stop!!

Finally, Rex runs away, yelping with his tail between his legs. All the other children start to laugh.

KID #2
Ha, ha! I'm sure glad MY dog isn't gay!

KID #3
Yeah, maybe you should name your dog SparkETTE, Stan!

KID #2
Gay dog!

Stan looks at Sparky and sulks.

INT. CLASSROOM

Cartman is at the head of the class, giving what appears to be a book report.

CARTMAN
And so you see, Simon and Simon were not brothers in real life, only on television.

MR. GARRISON
Thank you for that presentation, Eric, but the assignment was on Asian cultures. You get a D-.

CARTMAN
Aw, dammit!

MR. GARRISON
Who should we call on next, Mr. Hat?

MR. HAT
Well how about Stan, our little South Park quarterback star?

MR. GARRISON
Oh, good idea. Okay, Stanley, you're next.

Stan gets up.

STAN
Umm... I'm not really prepared either.

MR. GARRISON
Well, just make something up like Eric did.

STAN
Okay... Uh... Asian culture has... plagued our fragile Earth for many years. We must end it -

MR. GARRISON
Excellent! A-.

CARTMAN
AY!

STAN
Wow, cool!

CARTMAN
Wait a minute! Why the hell does he get an A-?!

MR. GARRISON
Eric, Stanley just might lead our team to victory against the Middle Park Cowboys for the first time in decades, and we treat star athletes better, because they're better people.

CARTMAN
That's not fair!

MR. HAT
Life isn't fair, kiddo, get used to it.

CARTMAN
(To himself)
Stupid puppet.

The school bell rings. The kids all start to get up.

MR. GARRISON (cont'd)
Don't forget your assignments tonight, children. They're due tomorrow for everybody but Stan.

The kids all walk out, but Stan stays behind and walks up to Garrison's desk.

STAN
Mr. Garrison, can I ask you a question?

MR. GARRISON
Of course Stanley, what is it?

STAN
What's a... homosexual?

Mr. Garrison's eyes get a little wide, he takes a deep breath.

MR. GARRISON
Oh... Well, Stanley, I guess you came to the right person... Sit down.

Stan sits down, Mr. Garrison folds his hands.

MR. GARRISON
(Soft and calm)
Stanley... Gay people... Well, gay people are evil. Evil right down to their cold black hearts, which pump not blood like yours and mine, but rather a thick, vomitous oil that oozes through their rotten veins and clots in their pea-sized brains which becomes the cause of their Nazi-esque patterns of violent behavior. Do you understand?

STAN
I guess.

MR. GARRISON
Good, I'm glad we could have this little talk, Stanley. Now you go outside and practice football like a good little heterosexual.

Stan blinks.

EXT. BUS STOP

The boys get off the bus and head home.

CARTMAN
You see me block that defense today? I was kicking ass.

KYLE
You're gonna need to kick more ass than that to beat the Cowboys.

CARTMAN
Hey, speaking of pounding ass, here comes Stan's little homo dog.

STAN
Shut up, dude!

Sparky walks up wearing a pink scarf.

STAN
Sparky! Where'd you get that pink scarf?!

Sparky wags his tail. Stan grabs the scarf, pulls it off and tosses it away. Sparky barks extremely gayly.

SPARKY
(Feminine)
Bark, bark.

CARTMAN
Man, that is the gayest dog I have ever seen.

STAN
He just needs some training, that's all... Sit Sparky!

Sparky sits.

STAN
Good boy... Now, shake...

Sparky gives Stan his paw.

STAN
Good boy... Now, DON'T BE GAY.

Sparky cocks his head to one side.
Stan holds out a doggie snack.

STAN
DON'T BE GAY, Spark. DON'T BE GAY.

Sparky frowns.

KYLE
Did it work?

STAN
I dunno.

CARTMAN
He still looks pretty gay to me.

Some of the other kids walk by.

KID
Hey Stan, your dog been to any pride marches lately?

KID #2
Yeah, maybe you should take him to a
Barbra Streisand concert.

KID
Ha Ha, Yeah.

KID #2
Stupid little gay dog.

KID
Gay dog.

The mean kids walk away. Stan fumes.

STAN
Come on you guys, I have an idea!

SOUTH PARK

PAGE 46

100

Scene | Panel | BG

Location/Time

Dialogue

KYLE
Did it work?

STAN
I dunno.

CARTMAN
He still looks pretty gay to me.

Trans.

101

Scene | Panel | BG

Location/Time

Some of the other kids walk by.

KID
Hey Stan, your dog been to any pride marches lately?

KID 2
Yeah, maybe you should take him to a Barbara ~~Streisand~~ concert.

KID
Ha Ha Yea.

Trans.

cont.

CONTINUED:

101

Scene | Panel | BG

Location/Time *FRAMING

Dialogue

KID 2
Stupid little gay dog.

KID
Gay dog.

Action/Efx

The mean kids walk away. Stan fumes.

Trans.

* FRAME THIS THE SAME AS PREVIOUS

SOUTH PARK

PAGE 47

102

Scene | Panel | BG

Location/Time

Dialogue

STAN
Come on you guys, I have an idea!

Action/Efx

Trans.

103

Scene | Panel | BG

Location/Time EXT. SMALL WOODEN BUILDING (DAY)

Dialogue

Action/Efx

Jimbo and Ned walk up to the humble, small building and open the door.

Trans.

104

Scene | Panel | BG

Location/Time INT. SPORTS BAR

Dialogue

(9 monitors)

Action/Efx

The interior is ridiculously huge.

Like the sports ~~book at~~ Ceasars palace

Ned and Jimbo walk up to the booking counte

Trans.

* NEED VIDEO IMAGES IN T.V.'S.

EXT. SMALL WOODEN BUILDING

Jimbo and Ned walk up to the humble, small building and open the door.

INT. SPORTS BAR

The interior is ridiculously huge. Like the sports book at Ceasar's Palace.

Ned and Jimbo walk up to the booking counter.

JIMBO
I want five hundred dollars on the South Park Cows!

BOOKIE
Are you crazy?

JIMBO
No siree, I'm telling you I got the line. My nephew Stan is the best quarterback the school has ever seen. I GUARANTEE they'll beat the spread!!
Suddenly, all the South Park residents go crazy placing bets at the counter.

TOWNSPERSON #1
I'm gonna put all my money on the Cows!

TOWNSPERSON #2
I'll put three hundred on the Cows if they guarantee it.

TOWNSPERSON 3
Hey I wanna put some money on the Cows too!

TOWNSPERSON #1
He gurantees it?

JIMBO
Uh- Woa... Woa... Don't get TOO carried away, now... I...

The place is an absolute frenzy, everyone in South Park is betting their life savings.

TOWNSPERSON #3
You better be right about this, Jimbo.

JIMBO
(A little uneasy)
Huh, huh... yeah, don't, don't worry yourself.

NED
Are you sure Stan is that good?

JIMBO
(Quietly)
Not THAT sure... I think we better come up with a backup plan... Uh let's see. Hey Bookie, what's the half-time show gonna be?

BOOKIE
You haven't heard? John Stamos' older brother Richard Stamos is gonna sing 'Loving You'.

NED
I love that song.

JIMBO
'Loving You'?? THAT'S PERFECT!!! Come on Ned, Middle Park's gonna get a half-time show they'll never forget!

COMMERCIAL BREAK #1

EXT. STAN'S HOUSE - DAY

The boys and Sparky are standing next to a very large box.

STAN
Okay, Sparky, we got you a present. Now, why don't... Dammit Sparky, where do you keep getting this thing?!

Stan pulls the pink bandana off of Sparky and again tosses it away.

STAN
NO PINK BANDANA, SPARKY! BAD DOG!!

Sparky turns his head.

STAN
Now pay attention, Sparky...

Stan opens the box, and out walks a gorgeous white poodle, with pink ribbons in her ears and a sparkling diamond collar.

STAN
This is Fifi.

Fifi struts around and shakes her rump.

KYLE
Ooh la la!

Sparky actually starts to look interested! Fifi walks in front of him and Sparky slowly starts to follow her!

CARTMAN
There he goes!

STAN
Atta boy, Spark! Get her!

Sparky hops up on top of Fifi -

STAN
YES!!

- Sparky grabs Fifi's diamond collar with his teeth, rips it off, and throws it over his own head. Stan looks incredibly disappointed as Sparky struts around with his new jewelry.

STAN
AW CRAP!! Now what do I do?!

KYLE
Who cares if your dog is gay? Maybe it's not that bad.

CARTMAN
No way, dude! My mom says God hates gay people... That's why He smote the sodomies in France.

KENNY
Mph rmphrm rmph rmph.

STAN
I know, Mr. Garrison said that homosexuals are evil... But, but Sparky doesn't seem evil.

KYLE
Well, maybe Mr. Garrison is wrong. You should ask somebody else.

STAN
Like who?

INT. TELEVISION

NARRATOR
And now back to 'Jesus and Pals' on South Park Public Access.

INT. TELEVISION STUDIO - DAY

Jesus sits at a desk with his hands folded.

JESUS
Yea, many of you are seeking answers. And I am the way for you my children. Let's open the phone lines back up for some questions.

Jesus hits a button on the desk.

JESUS
Hello caller, you're on the air.

MAN
Yeah, is this Jesus?

JESUS
Yes my son.

MAN
This... this is Robert from Torrey Pines.
I called last week asking for advice on my ex-wife.

JESUS
Of course, Robert, how are things now?

MAN
Everything's much better, Jesus, she hasn't mouthed off since. I just wanted to thank you for the advice. Oh, and for dying for my sins, too. That was really nice of you.

JESUS
Blessed art thou, Robert. Next caller, you're on the air.

STAN
Uh, hi, Jesus? I have a dog... And he's...
Uh... He's a homosexual.

JESUS
My son, a lot of people have wondered what my stance on homosexuality is. So I'd like to state once and for all my true opinion. You see -

Suddenly, the image is replaced by a card that reads 'South Park Public Access'.

NARRATOR
That's all the time we have left for 'Jesus and Pals', now stay tuned for 'Marty's Movie Reviews'!

INT. STAN'S HOUSE - DAY

Stan angrily hangs up the phone.

STAN
DAMMIT!

KYLE
What'd he say?

STAN
I got cut off for Marty's stupid Movie Reviews!

CARTMAN
Oh 'Marty's Movie Reviews' are on?! Kick ass!!

Cartman leaves.

STAN
ISN'T THERE ANYBODY WHO CAN HELP ME?!?!
ISN'T THERE ANYBODY WHO CARES?!

KYLE
Come on, dude, we have to get to practice.

STAN
NO IT'S NOT OKAY!! I DON'T WANT A GAY DOG!!!

EXT. STAN'S HOUSE - DAY

Sparky is standing in his little fenced yard. He looks up at an open window in the house where he can hear Stan clearly.

STAN
I WANT A BUTCH DOG!! I WANT A RIN TIN TIN!!

Sparky lowers his head sadly. He turns, digs a quick little hole under the fence, and walks away. Sparky looks back only once, then makes his way out into the great unknown.

EXT. FOOTBALL FIELD - DAY

CHEF
Now children, we've got to handle the ball better.

The boys are all standing there holding footballs.

CHEF
You've got to hold your football like you would hold your lover.

The boys just stand there.

CHEF
Gently, yet firmly.

The boys blink. Funky music kicks in.

CHEF
You want to be both nurturing and clinging at the same time... Oh yeah... just like making sweet love to the football... Be naughty with the football -

CHEF
(singing)
Spank it, ever so gently. Just...

KYLE
Ah chef...

CHEF
Spank it! Spank it!

KYLE
CHEF!!!

CHEF
Spank the football, spank it.

KYLE
CHEF!!!!!

The music stops.

CHEF
Huh? Oh... Sorry, children... Let's run some plays.

The kids head for the field.

PIP
Ah, Mr. Chef, sir?

CHEF
No, Pip, we still don't have a helmet for you.

PIP
Right-o... But how about I'll use a helmet today, and one of the other children goes without?

CHEF
That wouldn't be very fair to the other children, now would it?

PIP
Um, no... I guess not.

EXT. BOMBSMITHS

A small wooden building with a sign that reads 'Carl's' and under that 'Bombs, Explosives, and accessories'.

INT. BOMBSMITHS

Jimbo and Ned are sitting at a small table looking at a small bomb.

JIMBO
What we want to do, Carl, is put a trigger on that bomb that makes it go off at a specific moment during half-time.

CARL
And what moment would that be?

JIMBO
Well, John Stomos' older brother is all set to sing 'Loving You' during half-time. We want that bomb to go off when he hits that high F.

CARL
What high F?

JIMBO
You know-
(Singing)
'Loving you, is easy 'cause you're beautiful... Doot'n Doot'n Doo Doo AAAAHHH!!!'

CARL
So you want it to trigger on the 'Doot'n Doo?'

JIMBO
No damnit the 'AAAHHHH!!'

CARL
(Hitting wrong note)
'Aaahhhh?'

NED
'Ahhhhhh!'

JIMBO
'AHHHHHH!'

CARL
'Ahhhhh!'

JIMBO
'Doot'n doot'n doo doo. Ahhh!'

NED
'Doot'n doot'n doo doo.'

JIMBO
You got it.

CARL
'Doot'n doot'n doo doo. Ahhhhh,' Uh yeah, okay.

EXT. FOOTBALL FIELD - DAY

Practice is over. The boys are taking off their uniforms.

CHEF
What's the matter, Stan? You seem down.

STAN
I just can't concentrate, 'cause my dog is gay.

CHEF
Well, you know what they say; you can't teach a gay dog straight tricks.

MR. GARRISON
Oh, stop filling his head with that queer-loving propaganda.

CHEF
Say what? You of all people should be sympathetic.

MR. GARRISON
What do you mean?

CHEF
Well you're gay, aren't you?

MR. GARRISON
WHAT?! WHAT THE HELL ARE YOU TALKING ABOUT?! I am not gay!

CHEF
Well you sure do act like it.

MR. GARRISON
I just act that way to get chicks, dumbass.

Chef blinks.

KYLE
What's the matter, dude?

STAN
I don't know where Sparky is. He usually follows me to football practice.

CARTMAN
Maybe he went shopping for some leather pants.

Stan slugs Cartman in the head.

CARTMAN
OW!!

EXT. OUTSKIRTS OF SOUTH PARK

All alone in a vast blizzard, Sparky trudges on. He walks slowly and sadly. He turns his head one way, and then another, uncertain where to go. Finally, he spots a large structure and walks towards it. The sign slowly becomes visible. It reads 'Big Gay Al's'.

EXT. BIG AL'S

Sparky walks up to large wooden doors, from where a large gay man emerges.

BIG GAY AL
Hello there, little pup. I'm Big Gay Al.

Sparky looks around.

BIG GAY AL
Have you been outcast?

Sparky gives a little nod.

BIG GAY AL
Well then I'm so glad you found my big gay animal sanctuary. We're all big gay friends here. Would you like to live with us?

Sparky seems to smile.

BIG GAY AL
Come on in, little fellow.
Nobody will ever oppress you here...

Sparky Follows Big Gay Al into the large wooden doors.

EXT. BUS STOP - THE NEXT DAY

Stan walks up to the other boys.

STAN
Have you guys seen Sparky? He still hasn't come back.

KYLE
Wow, it's been like two days.

STAN
I think he might have run away.

CARTMAN
Did you check the shopping mall?

Stan slugs Cartman in the head.

CARTMAN
OW!

KYLE
Well, we'll help you look for him after the game.

STAN
I'm not playing.

KYLE
You what?

STAN
I'm not playing in that stupid game. I have to find my dog.

Stan walks away.

EXT. MIDDLE PARK ELEMENTARY - DAY

Middle Park is a much nicer, larger school. Jimbo and Ned quietly tiptoe around the exterior of the school. Ned is carrying the bomb.

JIMBO
Come on, Ned, and keep quiet.

NED
Okay.

They walk up to a little fenced-in horse. A sign above it reads 'Middle Park Cowboys Mascot - 'Enrique"

JIMBO
Hello there, Enrique.

NED
What are we doing here?

JIMBO
Well, Ned, we always kidnap Middle Park's mascot... But THIS year we're gonna booby-trap it instead!

Jimbo attaches the bomb to the horse.

JIMBO
And when John Stamos' older brother hits that high F in 'Loving You' BOOM!! No more Middle Park players!!

Jimbo and Ned laugh. The horse looks extremely worried.

JIMBO
God damn I love football!

EXT. OUTSIDE OF SOUTH PARK

Stan walks along looking for Sparky.

STAN
Sparky! Where are you??!!

Stan stops and looks around.

STAN
Where could he be?!

EXT. FOOTBALL FIELD - FIGHT

Now a large crowd has gathered at the football field. The Middle Park Cowboys, looking sharp in silver and blue uniforms, warm up for the game by doing stretches.

SPORTSCASTER FRANK
Hello everyone, this is Frank Hammond at South Park public radio AM 900, welcome to tonight's match up between the Middle Park Cowboys and the South Park Cows. Well, looks like Chef, the South Park Cows' coach is a little nervous... This is probably because his star quarterback has yet to show up.

CHEF
(nervously checking his watch)
Come on, Stan...

PIP
Uh, Mr. Chef, if Stanley doesn't show up, can I use his helmet?

CHEF
No, Pip, I'm sorry.

EXT. SOUTH PARK

Stan looks tired and beaten as he walks through the frozen tundra of South Park.

STAN
Sparky?! SPAAAARKY?!

COMMERCIAL BREAK #2

EXT. FOOTBALL FIELD - NIGHT

REFEREE
PLAY BALL!!

CHEF
You're gonna have to quarterback, Kyle.

KYLE
But I never practiced quarterback.

CHEF
Well it's a little late for that bullcrap now.

The ref blows his whistle and the kids head for the field.

SPORTSCASTER FRANK
Filling in for quarterback is number 12, Kyle Broslofski.

The townspeople all MOAN and GASP.

MR. GARRISON
Hey, hey, where's little Stanley?

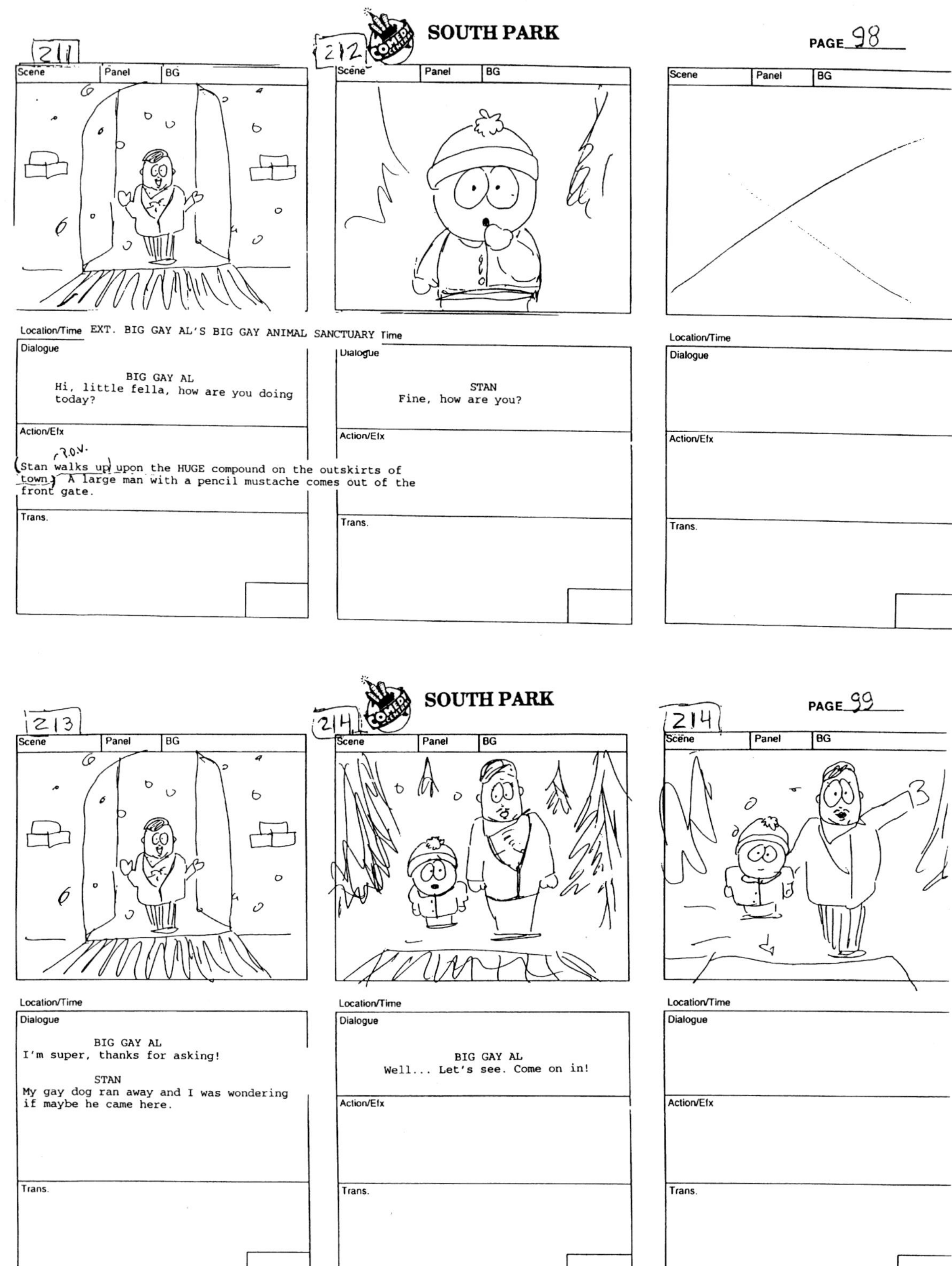

SOUTH PARK

PAGE 98

211

Scene | Panel | BG

Location/Time EXT. BIG GAY AL'S BIG GAY ANIMAL SANCTUARY Time

Dialogue

BIG GAY AL
Hi, little fella, how are you doing today?

Action/Efx

(Stan walks up) upon the HUGE compound on the outskirts of town.) A large man with a pencil mustache comes out of the front gate.

P.O.V.

Trans.

212

Scene | Panel | BG

Dialogue

STAN
Fine, how are you?

Action/Efx

Trans.

Scene | Panel | BG

Location/Time

Dialogue

Action/Efx

Trans.

SOUTH PARK

PAGE 99

213

Scene | Panel | BG

Location/Time

Dialogue

BIG GAY AL
I'm super, thanks for asking!

STAN
My gay dog ran away and I was wondering if maybe he came here.

Trans.

214

Scene | Panel | BG

Location/Time

Dialogue

BIG GAY AL
Well... Let's see. Come on in!

Action/Efx

Trans.

214

Scene | Panel | BG

Location/Time

Dialogue

Action/Efx

Trans.

MR. HAT
Yeah, why the hell is that little Jewish kid playing quarterback?!

Jimbo and Ned look at each other worriedly.

JIMBO
Ned! Look!

Jimbo points to the Middle Park sidelines, where Enrique is just barely visible in a little cage. Strapped around Enrique's torso, is the large, obvious bomb.

JIMBO
They've got Enrique on their sidelines! And it looks like that bomb is still attached!

NED
Yeah!

Jimbo and Ned rejoice.

EXT. BIG GAY AL'S BIG GAY ANIMAL SANCTUARY

Stan walks up upon the HUGE compound on the outskirts of town. A large man with a pencil mustache comes out of the front gate.

BIG GAY AL
Hi, little fella, how are you doing today?

STAN
Fine, how are you?

BIG GAY AL
I'm super, thanks for asking!

STAN
My gay dog ran away and I was wondering if maybe he came here.

BIG GAY AL
Well... Let's see. Come on in!

Big Gay Al whisks Stan inside the compound.

EXT. BIG GAY AL'S BIG GAY ANIMAL SANCTUARY

A huge outdoor compound with swimming pools and volleyball sandpits and every animal imaginable.

STAN
Do you have lots of gay dogs here?

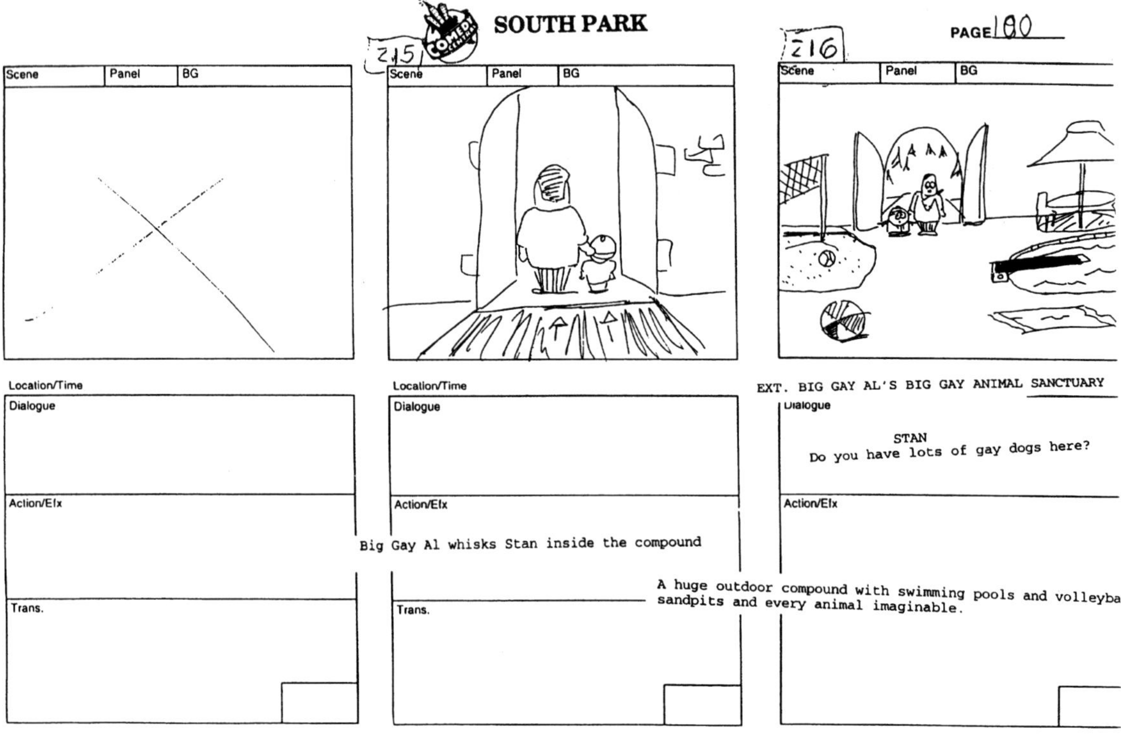
SOUTH PARK
PAGE 100
215
216
Scene
Panel
BG
Location/Time
EXT. BIG GAY AL'S BIG GAY ANIMAL SANCTUARY
Dialogue
STAN
Do you have lots of gay dogs here?
Action/Efx
Big Gay Al whisks Stan inside the compound
A huge outdoor compound with swimming pools and volleyba
sandpits and every animal imaginable.
Trans.

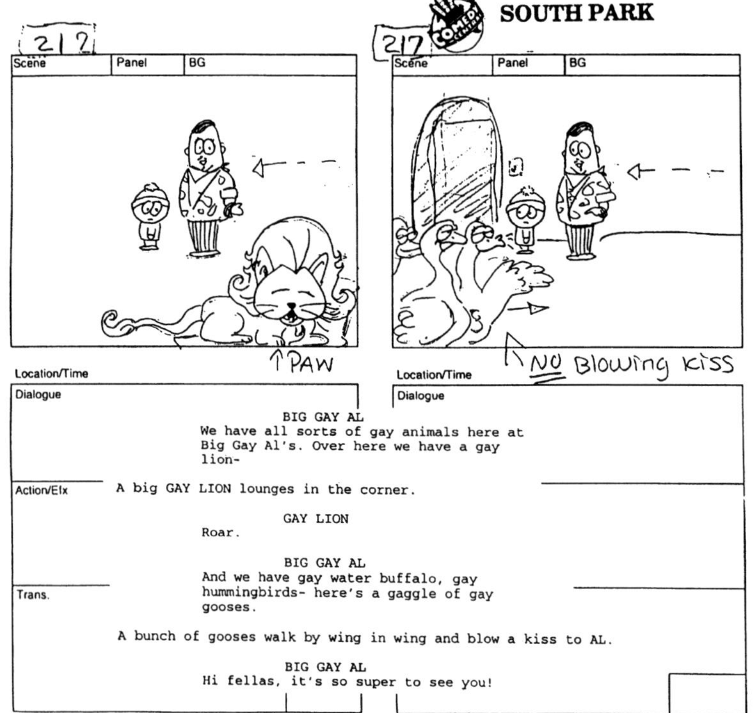
SOUTH PARK
217
217
Scene
Panel
BG
↑PAW
↑NO Blowing kiss
Location/Time
Dialogue
BIG GAY AL
We have all sorts of gay animals here at
Big Gay Al's. Over here we have a gay
lion-
Action/Efx
A big GAY LION lounges in the corner.
GAY LION
Roar.
BIG GAY AL
And we have gay water buffalo, gay
hummingbirds- here's a gaggle of gay
gooses.
Trans.
A bunch of gooses walk by wing in wing and blow a kiss to AL.
BIG GAY AL
Hi fellas, it's so super to see you!

PAGE 101
218
Scene
Panel
BG
Location/Time
Dialogue
STAN
Wow, it seems like the animals here are
really happy.
BIG GAY AL
Of course they are silly buns! It's the
one place where gay animals can really be
themselves. Do you like to dance?
Trans.

BIG GAY AL
We have all sorts of gay animals here at Big Gay Al's. Over here we have a gay lion -

A big GAY LION lounges in the corner.

GAY LION
Roar.

BIG GAY AL
And we have gay water buffalo, gay hummingbirds - here's a gaggle of gay gooses.

A bunch of gooses walk by wing in wing and blow a kiss to AL.

BIG GAY AL
Hi fellas, it's so super to see you!

STAN
Wow, it seems like the animals here are really happy.

BIG GAY AL
Of course they are, silly buns! It's the one place where gay animals can really be themselves. Do you like to dance?

Big Gay Al hits a switch on the wall and raging TECHNO music kicks in. All the animals start to gyrate.

EXT. FOOTBALL FIELD - NIGHT

The South Park team is in a huddle.

KYLE
Cartman, you hike me the ball. Then somebody run and I'll throw it or something. Ready...

PLAYERS
BREAK!

The kids step up to the line of scrimmage and look over the ominous Middle Park players.

MIDDLE PARK PLAYER
You guys are toast.

MIDDLE PARK PLAYER #2
Yeah! We're gonna pound your heads in!

CARTMAN
We'll just see about that!

Kyle gets behind Cartman, Cartman gets ready to hike the ball.

SOUTH PARK
PAGE 102
219
Scene
Panel
BG
Location/Time
Dialogue
Action/Efx
Big Gay Al hits a switch on the wall and raging TECHNO music kicks in. All the animals start to gyrate.
220
*Special set up
EXT. FOOTBALL FIELD - NIGHT
The South Park team is in a huddle.
Trans.
221
KYLE
Cartman you hike me the ball. Then somebody run and I'll throw it or something. Ready..
PLAYERS
BREAK!
SOUTH PARK
PAGE 118
258
SPORTSCASTER FRANK
It's taken by number 23...
259
SPORTSCASTER FRANK
Kenny McKormik.
Kenny grabs the ball and runs down the field. He actually manages to dodge some tacklers!
He runs faster and faster! He just might make a good play!
260
SPORTSCASTER FRANK (cont'd)
He's at the 50! The 40!
* A cowboy jumps for Kenny
Kenny stops & jumps over as another cowboy dives for Kenny - Kenny barely escapes

KYLE
Set... Set...

Cartman farts.

KYLE (cont'd)
DAMMIT CARTMAN!!

Suddenly Kyle backs off.

CHEF
(Shouting)
What's the matter?!

KYLE
Cartman farted!

CARTMAN
No I didn't! That was just my shoes.

Chef rolls his eyes.

CHEF
Come on, Kyle, we'll get a delay of game penalty!

KYLE
No way, dude!

CHEF
HIKE THE BALL!!

KYLE
Oh, dude, weak.

Kyle lifts his jersey up over his nose and gets back behind Cartman.

CARTMAN
That's right, you get back there now.

KYLE
HIKE!

The ball snaps.

SPORTSCASTER FRANK
The ball is snapped... Middle Park blitzes!!

The Middle Park kids charge Kyle and pound the shit out of him.

SPORTSCASTER FRANK (cont'd)
FUMBLE!! Middle Park gets the ball... They run it in for a TOUCHDOWN!! The score is seven - nothing Middle Park with 14:57 remaining in the first quarter.

In the stands, Ned and Jimbo look
at each other with concern.

JIMBO
Hell's bells.

SPORTSCASTER FRANK
I haven't seen a beating like that since Rodney King.

Sportscaster Phil quickly covers the microphone.

SPORTSCASTER PHIL
Now Frank, that's not very P.C. you're
gonna get in trouble again!

SPORTSCASTER FRANK
Right, right, I gotta watch that...

TOWNSPERSON
If we lose our money 'cause of your nephew,
we're gonna hang you up to dry, Jimbo!

JIMBO
Don't ya'll worry... You just wait 'til half-time!

INT. BIG GAY AL'S BIG GAY ANIMAL SANCTUARY

The animals continue to dance. Stan dances techno with
them, when suddenly he spots something.

STAN
SPARKY!!

SPARKY
Bark.

Sparky walks over with his pink bandana,
happy to see Stan.

STAN
Hiya Sparky, how's it going?

SPARKY
Bark.

STAN
I missed you, old pal, you really had me scared.

SPARKY
Bark.

STAN
Come on, let's go home, I can still make
it in time for the game.

Sparky starts to follow Stan out.

STAN
We can work on making you not gay together.

Sparky stops in his tracks.
Stan turns back around, puzzled.

STAN
Sparky?

Just then, Big Gay Al walks up behind Stan.

BIG GAY AL
Young man it appears you still don't understand.

STAN
What don't I understand?

BIG GAY AL
Come this way, I have to show you something.

EXT. FOOTBALL FIELD - NIGHT

ANNOUNCER
With just over a minute to go in the half, the score is Middle Park Cowboys 52, South Park Cows 0.

Kyle again hikes the ball, he hands off to Pip, whose head is a bloody, dirty mass. Pip charges the line of scrimmage and is immediately pummeled. One of the Cowboys scoops up the ball and runs it in for a touchdown.

SPORTSCASTER FRANK
I haven't seen an Englishman take a blow like that since Hugh Grant.

SPORTSCASTER PHIL
(Covering the mic)
Dude! Now that is NOT COOL!

SPORTSCASTER FRANK
Sorry, sorry.

INT. BIG GAY AL'S

Stan follows Big Gay Al through a large corridor.

BIG GAY AL
Okay Stan, I think you should get in line for my Big Gay Boat Ride.

SOUTH PARK
PAGE 119
261
Scene
Panel
BG
Location/Time
Dialogue
SPORTSCASTER FRANK
The 30!
Action/Efx
Trans.
262
Scene
Panel
BG
23
Location/Time
Dialogue
Action/Efx
Suddenly, two Middle Park players tackle Kenny, violently ripping off one of his arms. Kenny starts bleeding profusely, then gets his head ripped off by another Cowboy player.
Trans.
262 cont.
Scene
Panel
BG
23
pan over to head
Location/Time
Dialogue
pan over following Kenny's head
Action/Efx
Trans.
RATS Get Kenny
SOUTH PARK
PAGE 120
263
Scene
Panel
BG
Location/Time
Dialogue
SPORTSCASTER FRANK (cont'd)
OH MY!! The little running back is KILLED! I think he's... Yes he's been decapitated!
Action/Efx
Trans.
264
Scene
Panel
BG
12
Location/Time
Dialogue
KYLE
OH MY GOD! THEY'VE KILLED KENNY! YOU BASTARDS!!
Action/Efx
Trans.
265
Scene
Panel
BG
Location/Time
Dialogue
SPORTSCASTER PHIL
That's gotta hurt, Frank!
SPORTSCASTER FRANK
Ouch-a-roo! Looks like the South Park Cows aren't even going to beat the 72 point spread, not by a long shot.
Trans.

Big Gay Al points to a Disneyland-esque ride with 'Big Gay Al's Big Gay Boat Adventure' sign above it. Little wooden boats travel along a man-made canal, similar to the Jungle Cruise. About four people are standing in line.

BIG GAY AL (cont'd)
Step aboard, Stanley.

Stan and Big Gay Al get on one of the little boats, which heads down the canal. Big Gay Al picks up a microphone at the front of the boat.

BIG GAY AL (cont'd)
Hello everyone, and welcome aboard the Big Gay Boat Ride. On this adventure, we'll be seeing the world of gayness throughout time.

Stan blinks.

INT. FOOTBALL FIELD - NIGHT

The Cowboys kick off the ball to the Cows.

SPORTSCASTER FRANK
And the South Park Cows are set to receive... There's the kick... It's taken by number 23, Kenny McKormik.

Kenny grabs the ball and runs down the field. He actually manages to dodge some tacklers!

He runs faster and faster! He just might make a good play!

SPORTSCASTER FRANK (cont'd)
He's at the 50! The 40! The 30!

Suddenly, two Middle Park players tackle Kenny, violently ripping off one of his arms. Kenny starts bleeding profusely, then gets his head ripped off by another Cowboy player.

SPORTSCASTER FRANK (cont'd)
The little running back is DOWN! I think he's... Yes he's been decapitated!

KYLE
OH MY GOD! THEY'VE KILLED KENNY! YOU BASTARDS!!

SPORTSCASTER PHIL
That's gotta hurt, Frank!

SPORTSCASTER FRANK
Ouch-a-roo!

CHEF
Hey, come on, that was roughing!!...
At least let us scrape him off the field!!

SPORTSCASTER FRANK
Looks like the South Park Cows aren't even going to beat the 72-point spread, not by a long shot.

INT. BIG GAY AL'S

BIG GAY AL (cont'd)
You see, gayness has existed since the beginning of time...

The boat passes little animatronic cave men. Two of the cave men are holding hands.

BIG GAY AL (cont'd)
From the Egyptian Pharaohs...

The boat passes two gay Egyptian men.

BIG GAY AL
To the Shoguns of Japan...

Two Shoguns in a techno dance club.

BIG GAY AL (cont'd)
Oh, oh! Look out! It's the oppressors! Christians and Republicans and Nazis! OH MY!

Three lame animatronics dressed respectively as a Christian, a Republican and a Nazi, beat an innocent homosexual with a pipe.

Just like the Jungle Cruise, Big Gay Al takes out a fake pistol and fires blanks at the animatronics.

BIG GAY AL (cont'd)
Hoo! Oh gosh that was close! Okay let's steer our big gay boat out of here, and into a place where gays are allowed to live freely...

The boat passes through to large doors, which open into a HUGE, colorful, festive room where tons of animatronics dance and sing merrily.

SONG
'We're all gay and it's okay! 'Cause gay means happy and happy means gay! We're not sad anymore 'cause we're out the closet door! It's OKAY to be GAY!!'

Stan looks around in disbelief.
All the gay things dance, sing and do silly things.

SONG
'It's okay to be gay!
It's okay to be gay!
La La La La La...'

BIG GAY AL
So what do you think, Stan?

STAN
This kicks ass!

Stan looks down at Sparky.

STAN
I'm sorry I tried to change you, Spark.
I just didn't understand.

Sparky barks and pants happily.
Stan pets him on the head.

BIG GAY AL
Isn't this precious?

EXT. FOOTBALL FIELD - HALF-TIME - NIGHT

SPORTSCASTER FRANK
And now here to sing the touching song 'Loving You'
is the one and only... John Stamos' brother!!!

The crowd lets out a small smattering of applause.
Music begins. Jimbo and Ned give each other knowing
glances and then look over at the Middle Park sidelines.

ANGLE - SIDELINES

Enrique is absolutely horrified, waiting to explode in
the midst of the Middle Park players.

RESUME - FOOTBALL FIELD

Patrick Stamos steps up to the mic and starts to sing.

JOHN STAMOS' BROTHER
'Loving you... Is easy 'cause you're beautiful...'

ANGLE - JIMBO AND NED

ANGLE - ENRIQUE

RESUME - FOOTBALL FIELD

JOHN STAMOS' BROTHER
'Doo doo doot'n da doo...'

And then the big note is about to come...

JOHN STAMOS' BROTHER
(Low register)
'Ahhha...Ahhhh...Ahhhhh.'

Jimbo and Ned look shocked.

JIMBO
What the hell?!
He didn't sing the high F!!!

MR. GARRISON
Patrick Stamos can't sing a high F.
He always screws it up like this.

Jimbo and Ned look absolutely defeated.

JIMBO
Ned... We're gonna get our asses kicked.

JOHN STAMOS' BROTHER
'Loving you...'

MR. GARRISON
(heckling)
It's obvious where all the talent in THAT family went!

JOHN STAMOS' BROTHER
'Doot'n doot'n doo doo...'

COMMERCIAL BREAK #3

EXT. BIG GAY AL'S BIG GAY ANIMAL SANCTUARY

Stan, Sparky and Big Gay Al stand
outside the Animal Sanctuary.

STAN
Thanks for everything Big Gay Al!

SPARKY
Bark!!

BIG GAY AL
No problem kids! Are you sure you don't wanna stay for
some toasted cheese sandwiches?

STAN
No thanks, I've gotta get back for the
big football game. Come on boy!

Stan and Sparky run off.

BIG GAY AL
Oh Stan -

Stan turns around.

BIG GAY AL (cont'd)
When you get back to town... Tell them about us, will you? Tell them there are gay animals here who need homes desperately.

STAN
I will Big Gay Al, I will.

Stan waves goodbye and runs off. Big Gay Al watches Stan go fondly, and then suddenly panics.

BIG GAY AL
Ooh, my carrot cake!

EXT. FOOTBALL FIELD - NIGHT

The little football-clad kids crash violently into each other.

SPORTSCASTER FRANK
And these South Park Cows are being absolutely MOLESTED by Middle Park. I haven't seen so many children molested since -

In the stands, the townspeople are just sitting there, bored and disheartened.

MR. GARRISON
I thought you said beating the spread was a sure thing, Jimbo!

MR. HAT
Yeah, we all put our lives' savings in this game!

TOWNSPERSON #1
You're a DEAD MAN, Jimbo!!

Jimbo shrinks in his seat as all the townspeople start YELLING at him and throwing their food at him.

SPORTSCASTER FRANK
Well, this should just about wrap it up for - Wait a minute, what's this?

Suddenly, Stan and Sparky come running over the hill. The townspeople all CHEER!!

SPORTSCASTER PHIL
It's Stan, the South Park star quarterback!!

CHEF
Where the hell have you been, Stan?

STAN
I've been getting my best friend back.

Sparky pants happily.

CHEF
Just get in there, boy!

Chef throws a helmet on Stan's head and pats his ass toward the playing field.

JIMBO
Give 'em hell, Stanley!!

Stan walks up to the line of scrimmage.

JIMBO
(Praying)
Jesus... Now I haven't asked you for much... But all we need is one little score. PLEASE? PLEASE Jesus??

Pull back to reveal that Jesus is sitting next to him in the stands.

JESUS
Leave me alone.

STAN
HIKE!

SPORTSCASTER FRANK
Stan hikes the ball... He steps back to pass!!

KYLE
Hey Stan! I'm open I think!!

SPORTSCASTER FRANK
And he throws it to Kyle, the little Jewish kid!

Kyle catches the ball and runs down the field.

SPORTSCASTER FRANK (cont'd)
Oh my! I haven't seen a Jew run like that since Poland, 1938!

SPORTSCASTER PHIL
DUDE!!

Kyle runs into the end zone and falls down.

SPORTSCASTER PHIL
TOUCHDOWN!!!!!

The crowd goes wild.

SPORTSCASTER FRANK
The clock runs out! And the final score is Middle Park Cowboys 73, South Park Cows six! South Park beats the spread.

Everybody cheers and hugs. The South Park Cows all converge on Stan and rejoice. Stan is heroically hoisted onto a small stage, where everybody is gathered around.

TOWNSPERSON
Speech!

Sportscaster Frank steps up and shoves a microphone in front of Stan.

SPORTSCASTER FRANK
Stan, what do you want to tell the world about this stunning almost victory?

STAN
Uh... It... It's really cool that we beat the spread against the Cowboys.

The townspeople all cheer.

STAN
And... And maybe we can beat 'em even more next year!

The townspeople all cheer.

STAN
And it's okay to be gay!

The townspeople all get incredibly quiet.

JIMBO
What?!

STAN
Being gay is just a part of nature, and a beautiful thing!

MR. GARRISON
What the hell is he talking about?!

SPORTSCASTER FRANK
Uh... Stanley you arrived very late in the game, where were you that whole time?

STAN
I was with my new friend Big Gay Al. He showed me his Big Gay Animal Sanctuary and took me on a Big Gay Boat Ride where I learned all about the wonders of gayety.

The townspeople all look at each other and blink.

STAN
It's true, I'll show you.

EXT. BIG GAY AL'S BIG GAY ANIMAL SANCTUARY

Nestled between the two mountain peaks are...
Nothing. No Big Gay Al's... Nothing.

STAN
But it was here... It was all right here.
There was a techno dance club...

CARTMAN
Stan, you need to lay off the cough syrup, alright,
seriously I'm worried about you man.

TOWNSPERSON
OLIVER!!

A townsperson runs over to where all the gay animals are standing and picks up a cat.

TOWNSPERSON
I thought you ran away all those months ago!

Now other townspeople walk toward the gay animals and start to reunite.

TOWNSPERSON #2
SIDNEY!!

TOWNSPERSON #3
WHINNY!!

TOWNSPERSON #4
CARLOS!!

The townspeople all rejoice with their gay animals, leaving Stan all alone.

BIG GAY AL
I want to thank you for bringing everybody here.

Big Gay Al is standing there with a small suitcase, which he sets on the ground and opens.

STAN
Oh, there you are, dude. How's it going?

BIG GAY AL
I'm super, thanks for asking.
It looks like now my work here is done.

Big Gay Al steps into his suitcase, and presses a large blue button.

BIG GAY AL (cont'd)
Goodbye, Stanley, peace be with you.

The suitcase closes with Big Gay Al inside, then powers up and shoots up into the sky to outer space.

STAN
Wow...

Stan watches as the little suitcase ship becomes just another twinkling star.

COMMERCIAL BREAK #4

JOHN STAMOS' BROTHER
YOU GUYS, YOU GUYS!! I CAN DO IT!!

Everybody looks at Patrick Stamos.

MR. GARRISON
Do what?

JOHN STAMOS' BROTHER
(Singing)
'Loving you... Is easy 'cause you're beautiful.
Doot'n Doot'n...'

Enrique looks absolutely horrified. Jimbo and Ned look even more horrified.

JIMBO
NO!!!

JOHN STAMOS' BROTHER
'Doo Doo! AA-'

BOOOOMMM!!

FIN

EPISODE 106

DEATH

BY TREY PARKER & MATT STONE

ACT I

INT. STAN'S HOUSE - DINING ROOM - NIGHT

Stan's family (Father, sister and grandfather) are seated at a table. Mother walks up holding a birthday cake with a ridiculous number of candles.

STAN & FAMILY
Happy birthday to you! Happy birthday to you!
Happy birthday dear Grandpa!

Grandpa drools a little from his wheelchair.

STAN & FAMILY (cont'd)
Happy birthday to you!

STAN'S MOTHER
Now blow out the candles, Grandpa!

Grandpa manages the smallest wheeze, which doesn't even make the flames of the candles flicker.

Stan's family members all applaud.

STAN'S FATHER
How does it feel to be a hundred and two, Paps?

GRANDPA
Shoot me.

STAN'S MOM
Make a wish, Grandpa!

GRANDPA
I wish I were dead.

FATHER
Ha, ha! That's our silly Grandpa!

GRANDPA
I'm not being silly! Kill me! I'd do it myself,
but I'm too damn old!

STAN'S MOM
Oh, who wants ice cream with their cake?

STAN
I will.

FATHER
Me.

Stan looks up at the clock and gasps.

STAN
It's eight o'clock! My favorite T.V. show is on!

SHELLEY
That show's for babies, it's so stupid!

STAN
Can I eat my cake in the living room, Mom? Please? Can I?

STAN'S MOM
Oh, alright. But take your grandpy with you.

STAN
Aw, dammit.

STAN'S MOM
Language!

INT. LIVING ROOM - CONTINUOUS

Stan is sitting on the couch watching television and eating cake.

NARRATOR
And now back to 'Terrance and Phillip'!

ANGLE - TELEVISION

Two average-looking teens (animated in a slightly different style) are sitting on a couch.

PHILLIP
Hey Terrance, I think I have to fart.

Stan laughs.

TERRANCE
Wait! before you do, pull my thumb.

Phillip pulls Terrance's thumb. Terrance FARTS loudly. The laugh track laughs. Stan laughs. PAN OVER to reveal Grandpa, who is trying to point a shotgun at his head. Grandpa pulls the trigger - BLAM!! He misses, blowing a picture off the wall.

GRANDPA
Aw dammit!!

Grandpa looks at Stan.

GRANDPA
How would you like to make a dollar, Billy?

STAN
My name's not Billy, Grandpa, it's Stan.

GRANDPA
Dammit, Billy! Do you want a dollar or don't ya?!

STAN
Sure.

GRANDPA
Okay, you just have to do one thing for me...

STAN
I'm not going to kill you, Grandpa.

GRANDPA
WHY NOT?!

STAN
'Cause! I'll get in trouble!

GRANDPA
I killed my grandpa when I was your age!

STAN
Leave me alone, Grandpa.

GRANDPA
What has America's youth come to?! Kids won't even kill their own grandparents!!

INT. KYLE'S HOUSE - NIGHT

Kyle is sitting in front of the T.V. watching the same T.V. show.

ANGLE - TELEVISION

PHILLIP
Hey Terrance, now that you've farted, I think I might fart too!

Phillip leans over and rips a big one. The laugh track laughs.

TERRANCE
Ooh! You farted!

The laugh track laughs again.

Kyle laughs painfully. He holds his stomach. Just then, Kyle's mother walks in.

KYLE'S MOTHER
Kyle boopie, what are you watching?

But Kyle is laughing too hard to speak. His mother looks at the television.

TERRANCE
Hey Phillip, would you like a flower?

PHILLIP
I sure would, Terrance.

TERRANCE
Alrighty then, here's a Tulip.

PUUU!! Terrance farts.

RESUME - KYLE AND MOTHER

Kyle is rolling around on the floor, laughing wildly.

KYLE'S MOTHER
What is this? It's horrible!

KYLE
(Collecting himself)
Dude, it's 'Terrance and Phillip'.

ANGLE - TELEVISION

PHILLIP
Take that you stupid dick!

KYLE'S MOTHER
WHAT did he say?!

TERRANCE
You're an asshole, Phillip!

KYLE'S MOTHER
What-what-WHAAAATT?

Kyle's mom snaps the T.V. off.

KYLE'S MOTHER
Young man, you are not to watch that show anymore!
It's immature toilet humor!

KYLE
But EVERYBODY watches 'Terrance and Phillip'!

KYLE'S MOTHER
Oh, really, is that SO?!

INT. CARTMAN'S HOUSE

Cartman is on the couch eating Cheesy Poofs
and watching television.

ANGLE - TELEVISION

Terrance and Phillip are floating out in space.

TERRANCE
Oh no, Phillip! looks like you're about to fart!

PHILLIP
You're exactly right, Terrance!!

A huge FART sound. Cartman laughs wildly.

CARTMAN
Sweet!

CARTMAN'S MOM
Eric dear, I just got a call from your friend Kyle's mother. She said that this show is naughty, and might make you a potty mouth.

CARTMAN
That's a bunch of crap. Kyle's mom is a dirty Jew.

CARTMAN'S MOM
Oh, okay hon.

INT. STAN'S HOUSE

Stan walks up to his bedroom door and looks at his list of chores. 'Take Out Trash' followed by 'Feed Sparky' then 'Clean Up Room' and then, sloppily scribbled in crayon, 'Kill Grandpa'.

Stan looks confused, then realizes that Grandpa is down the hall.

STAN
I'm not going to kill you, Grandpa!

Grandpa appears in the background.

GRANDPA
Ingrate!

STAN
G'night, Grandpa.

Stan goes into his room.

GRANDPA
You pompous son of a whore!

INT. CLASSROOM - DAY

The kids are filing into their desks.

Kyle gets into his desk, and immediately gets slugged in the head by Cartman.

KYLE
OW! What the hell was that for?!

CARTMAN
That's for your stupid mother! She made me miss 'Terrance and Phillip' last night!

CLYDE
Yeah, what's the big idea having your mom call all our moms last night?

KYLE
Well, I didn't have her do it, she did it on her own!

CARTMAN
Why does this happen every month? It seems like right about the same time every month Kyle's mom gets a hair up her ass about something - and I always end up getting screwed by it!

Mr. Garrison steps in front of the class.

MR. GARRISON
Children, children, a certain student's mother called me last night...

CARTMAN
Oh gee, I wonder whose mother THAT could have been!

MR. GARRISON
She informed me that some of you might be watching a naughty show called 'Terrance and Phillip'.

The whole class smiles and cheers.

CLASS
YEAH!

MR. HAT
Watching that show is bad, Mr. Garrison.

MR. GARRISON
That's right, Mr. Hat, shows like 'Terrance and Phillip' are what we call 'toilet humor'. They don't expand your minds.

The kids blink.

MR. GARRISON (cont'd)
You see, children, these kind of shows are senseless, vile trash.

Kenny walks in.

MR. GARRISON (cont'd)
Kenny, why are you late to class?

Kenny says nothing, but just hands Mr. Garrison a note.

ANGLE - NOTE

'Please excuse me for being late.
I have explosive diarrhea'.

RESUME - GARRISON

MR. GARRISON
Oh. Okay, Kenny. Be seated.

Kenny walks to his desk.

MR. GARRISON
Now, as I was saying, the reason that parents of South Park are so upset is because you - yes Kenny, what is it?

Kenny has his hand raised.

KENNY
Mph rmph rm.

MR. GARRISON
I thought you just came from the bathroom.

KENNY
Mph rm rmph rm mph mph rm rm mm.

MR. GARRISON
Oh okay, okay, go ahead.

Kenny walks into a little bathroom.

MR. GARRISON
As I was saying, you all seem to enjoy this show, even though it isn't based in reality. There is much more to life than two young men farting on each other.

Suddenly, we HEAR the sounds of splashing water and explosive diarrhea.

MR. GARRISON
And throughout history there have always been shows that have come and gone that have been very bad. Usually they get taken right off the air. You see you should be spending your time enlightening your mind with more intelligent entertainment.

Kenny walks out of the bathroom and takes his seat again.

STAN
Whew! Smells like you slaughtered a cow in there, Kenny!

MR. GARRISON
Pay attention, children! I'm going to join your parents in requesting that you don't watch 'Terrance and Phillip' anymore, ever.

CARTMAN
WHAT?!

CLYDE
Not watch 'Terrance and Phillip' EVER?

MR. GARRISON
That's right, children, are there any questions?
(Pause)
Yes, Stanley?

STAN
Is it okay to kill somebody if they want you to?

Garrison is taken aback.

MR. GARRISON
What do you mean?

The whole class sits and thinks.

STAN
My grandpa keeps asking that I kill him all the time, and sometimes I wonder if I should.

KYLE
Well then you should. I think that a person has a right to die if they wanna.

STAN
Really?

KYLE
Yeah, there's this guy named Jack Laborkian that goes around and murders people that ask him to, and he doesn't get in trouble at all.

STAN
Wow.

CARTMAN
Hey! Maybe we could get him to kill Kyle's mom!

STAN
So IS it okay to assist somebody with suicide,
Mr. Garrison?

Mr. Garrison thinks.

MR. GARRISON
Uh, Stan... I'm not touching that one with a
twenty-foot pole.

Stan looks bummed.

KENNY
Mph mph mph!!!

Kenny dashes to the bathroom, slams the door, and lets loose horrible, explosive diarrhea.

COMMERCIAL BREAK #1

INT. CAFETERIA - DAY

The boys are in line for lunch.

CARTMAN
Man, I can't believe we're gonna miss 'Terrance and
Phillip' today! I think I'm already having withdrawal!

Cartman starts shaking and quivering uncontrollably.

STAN
Don't worry, dude. We can all go watch it at my house!
My parents don't get home until late.

KYLE
But won't your grandpa be there?

STAN
Yeah...

CARTMAN
Just kill him, dude, maybe he'll give you some money.

CHEF
Hello there, children!

STAN
Hey Chef.

CHEF
How's it going?

STAN
Bad.

CHEF
Why bad?

STAN
Chef, is it okay to kill your grandpa?

CHEF
You can't kill my grandpa, Stan, he's already passed on.

STAN
No I mean kill MY grandpa.

CHEF
No I don't think that's okay, Stan. In fact I think that's illegal.

STAN
See, I told you, dude.

KYLE
Well yeah, but what if the grandpa wants to die, 'cause he's really old, and he's just asking for help?

CARTMAN
Yeah, like assisted suicide, what about that?

Chef thinks again.

CHEF
I don't want to touch that with a forty-foot pole.

Chef runs away.

The boys just sit there and blink.

STAN
What's the big deal? Why won't anybody talk about this?

INT. PTA MEETING - DAY

A large group of parents have gathered in a small meeting hall. Kyle's mother is at the head of the group, speaking at a podium.

KYLE'S MOTHER
... and I myself was not aware of this outrageous, horrible show until recently. I have a clip of this show to demonstrate exactly what I mean.

Kyle's mom hits a button of a remote. A video image of 'Terrance and Phillip' starts.

ANGLE - TELEVISION SCREEN

TERRANCE
Hey, Phillip, guess what?

PHILLIP
What?

FARRRRRRT...

The clip ends.

KYLE'S MOTHER
Now, apparently that's supposed to be FUNNY.

Laughing is heard from the back of the room.
CUT TO Stan's father, who is giggling to himself.

STAN'S DAD
Ha, ha... He farted right on his head!

The other parents look at Stan's dad, disgusted.

Kyle's mom sighs.

KYLE'S MOTHER
Not allowing our kids to watch this show is not enough.
We need to BOYCOTT THE ENTIRE NETWORK!! ALL
THOSE IN FAVOR?!

Hands bolt up into the air.

Suddenly, violent pooh sounds emerge from the toilet.

Mr. Garrison steps out.

MR. GARRISON
Ooh, I think I've caught a touch of flu from little Kenny
this morning. I've got the green apple splatters.
Some of the men in the audience laugh.

INT. STAN'S HOUSE

Stan walks in the door followed by the other boys.
Grandpa is sitting in his wheelchair trying to
stick a fork into a light socket.

STAN
Hi, Grandpa. I brought my friends
over to watch T.V. if that's okay.

GRANDPA
Billy, help Grandpa stick this fork in the outlet.

STAN
No Grandpa, I'll get in trouble!

GRANDPA
Kill me, God dammit!

STAN
No! I can't even kill a deer!

GRANDPA
Well then have one of your little friends do it!!
(To Cartman)
You can kill me, can't you?

CARTMAN
I would never kill somebody -
not unless they pissed me off.

GRANDPA
Oh, is that a fact? Well, let me tell you something,
Porky, your mom was over here earlier
and I humped her like a little bitch.

CARTMAN
WHAT?!

GRANDPA
That's right.

STAN
GRANDPA!!

GRANDPA
And then I dug up your great grandma's skeleton
and had my way with her too! Choice piece of ass,
your great grandma!!

CARTMAN
HEY! YOU PIECE OF CRAP! I'LL KILL YOU!!

GRANDPA
That's the spirit, Tubby!!

STAN
Come on, Cartman, he's just trying to get to you!

Stan grabs Cartman and pulls him away.

CARTMAN
Don't talk about my mom like that!!

STAN
We can go watch 'Terrance and Phillip' in the kitchen.

GRANDPA
(Calling after him)
I ever tell you 'bout the time I boofed your dad, Fatso?

INT. STAN'S HOUSE - KITCHEN

The boys are standing next to a small T.V. set and a phone. Cartman is still fuming.

CARTMAN
I can't believe that son of a bitch!

STAN
Here, Cartman, have some snacky cakes.

CARTMAN
(Suddenly fine)
Ooh, snacky cakes? Good deal...

Cartman starts to gorge himself.

STAN
I don't know what to do, dude.
My grandpa really wants to die.

KYLE
I'm telling you, it's okay.
Maybe you should ask the Lord for guidance.

STAN
Hey yeah, good idea.

Stan picks up the phone.

INT. 'JESUS AND PALS' SET

NARRATOR
And now back to 'Jesus and Pals' on
South Park Public Access.

JESUS
Yea, believe in me and ye shall find peace...
First caller, you're on 'Jesus and Pals'.

VOICE
Yeah, is this Jesus?

JESUS
Yes, caller, you need to turn your T.V. down,
that's why you're getting that weird feedback.

VOICE
Oh sorry... Uh, this is Mar-

JESUS
Martin from Aspen Park, yes I know.

VOICE
... How the hell did you know that?

JESUS
Well, maybe because I'm the son of God, Brainiac, now do you have a question?

VOICE
Oh yeah, uh, I have this cousin who cheated on the SATs to-

JESUS
Tell little Gregory that cheating is lying and lying is wrong, no matter what the circumstance.

VOICE
Oh, okay, thanks for the advice, Jesus.

JESUS
Next caller, you're on the air.

STAN
Jesus?

JESUS
Yes my son.

STAN
Jesus, is it okay to kill somebody if they ask you to because they're in a lot of pain? You know, like assisted suicide. Is that okay?

JESUS
My son...

STAN
Yes?

JESUS
I'm not touching that with a sixty-foot pole.

Jesus QUICKLY reaches over and switches phone lines.

JESUS
Next caller -

INT. STAN'S HOUSE

STAN
GOD DAMMIT!!

JESUS
I heard that.

STAN
What the hell is wrong with everybody?!

CARTMAN
Hey you guys! 'Terrance and Phillip' is on!

STAN
Yeah!

Stan starts to change the channel.

KYLE
Hey, do you think we'll get in trouble for watching it?

STAN
Kyle, don't be a butthole!

CARTMAN
Yeah, just 'cause your mom is a stupid bitch doesn't mean the whole world has to suffer.

KYLE
Don't call my mom a bitch, Cartman!

CARTMAN
Oh, bitch... your mom is a bitcha bitcha bitch...

ANGLE - TELEVISION

ANNOUNCER
And now back to 'Terrance and Phillip'.

The two very plain looking teens are sitting on a couch.

TERRANCE
Hey Philip, would you like to eat some beans?

PHILLIP
Oh yeah! I love beans!

RESUME - KITCHEN

CARTMAN
(Laughing)
Oh oh... I bet I know what's coming!

Grandpa wheels himself in and nonchalantly hands Stan a piece of rope.

GRANDPA
Billy, would you mind holding this for Grandpa, please?

Stan doesn't take his eyes off the T.V.

STAN
Okay, Grandpa, okay. Just get out of the way of the T.V.

Stan takes the rope. Grandpa heads to the background.

ANGLE - TELEVISION

TERRANCE
Hey Phillip, it looks like those beans might make me fart!

PHILLIP
Well, don't fart on me, Terrance!

RESUME - LIVING ROOM

The boys all laugh merrily. Meanwhile, Grandpa is doing something odd in the background.

He is throwing the other end of the rope around a crossbeam.

KYLE
Dude, he's gonna fart on his head again!!

Suddenly, Kenny jumps up and rushes to the bathroom. We HEAR a door SLAM and then the sounds of splashing water and explosive diarrhea.

KENNY
Mmmf Mrph mamm Mrmmm!

CARTMAN
Hey, you're gonna miss it, Kenny!

A fart sound comes from the T.V. The boys all break out laughing hysterically.

PHILLIP
You're such an ASSHOLE Terrance!!

TERRANCE
Ha Ha charade I am.

The boys laugh even harder.

CARTMAN
Hurry up, Kenny! You're gonna miss the fart!!

Just then, Shelley walks in!

SHELLEY
JESUS CHRIST! WHAT THE HELL ARE YOU DOING?!?!

Stan jumps up and stands in front of the T.V.

STAN
We're not watching 'Terrance and Phillip', I swear! I mean... CARTMAN was watching it.

SHELLEY
No, I mean what the HELL ARE YOU DOING TO GRANDPA?!

Stan looks down at the rope in his hand, then follows it up over a crossbeam, and finally sees Grandpa at the other end, hanging by the neck.

GRANDPA
(Choking)
Tug... a... little... harder... Billy...

STAN
AGH!

Stan lets go of the rope and Grandpa crashes to the ground.

SHELLEY
You little jerk, you were trying to kill Grandpa!! I'm telling Mom!!

GRANDPA
(Coughing)
Dammit, I was so close!

INT. NEWSROOM - DAY

REPORTER
Four third graders from South Park, Colorado were found trying to viciously murder an innocent grandfather.

INT. STUDIO - DAY

The boys are on some kind of talk show.

REPORTER
Boys, how did you get driven so far to the edge? What changed you into such demonic little bastards?

STAN
We didn't know what we were doing. We were just sitting there watching 'Terrance and Phillip' and -

REPORTER
'Terrance and Phillip'!! Ah HA!!! SO it IS that show that is to blame!

EXT. SOUTH PARK

Kyle's mother is standing in front of the town with yet another reporter.

KYLE'S MOTHER
These boys' minds have been tainted by the garbage on television that they see, and we are FED UP!

A random TOWNSPERSON holds his stomach and runs into a bathroom where thundering shit sounds emerge. Garrison runs up to the bathroom door and pounds on it.

KYLE'S MOTHER
We have to stop this smut from going on the air! We will march to the network and PROTEST UNTIL OUR DEMANDS ARE MET!! NEW YORK, HERE WE COME!!!

The parents all cheer.

COMMERCIAL BREAK #2

ACT II

EXT. NEW YORK

Establishing shot of the filthy, violent, rancid city that is New York.

EXT. CARTOON CENTRAL - DAY

Within the city, a mob is gathered out front of the towering skyscraper of Cartoon Central. Kyle's mother stands in front of the crowd with a bullhorn, addressing the crowd.

KYLE'S MOTHER
We are spreading the word to this establishment - That we DEMAND better television for our children!

The people cheer.

KYLE'S MOTHER (cont'd)
We want more QUALITY television like 'Full House'!!

Several of the South Park residents, however, are waiting in line for one of the two port-o-potties.

STAN'S FATHER
Ooh, I think you gave me the stomach flu, Mr. Garrison.

MR. GARRISON
No, no, it was that little Kenny bastard that gave it to me.

Mayor McDaniels steps out.

STAN'S DAD
Woa, Mayor, you making gravy in there?

MAYOR McDANIELS
I just had a brown baby boy!

They all laugh, in spite of themselves.

INT. STAN'S HOUSE

The boys are running around the house like crazy. Garbage and food is everywhere.

KYLE
Dude! This is SWEET not having any parents around!

STAN
Yeah! I hope they protest T.V. shows forever!

The boys start jumping up and down on the sofa.

STAN
WHOOPEE!!!!

GRANDPA
Come here, Billy, I want to show you something...

STAN
Aw, do I have to?

GRANDPA
Yes you do you little pecker!

Stan sighs and follows his grandfather.

GRANDPA
I realized that the reason you won't kill me, is because you don't understand how I feel, Billy.

They walk to one of the bedroom doors.

GRANDPA
But I found out a way to show YOU what it feels like to be Grandpa.

INT. STAN'S HOUSE - GUEST BEDROOM

Grandpa leads Stan into a little bedroom and closes the door, locking both himself and Stan inside.

STAN
Hey, what are you doing?

Grandpa hits a switch, and the lights in the room go out. Stan tries to look around the dark room.

Grandpa reaches down and puts a tape into a tape player.

EXT. STAN'S HOUSE - HALLWAY

The other boys have their ears pinned against the door.

KYLE
What are they doing in there?

CARTMAN
I don't know...

INT. STAN'S HOUSE - GUEST BEDROOM

GRANDPA
Now, you're about to see what it's like to be as old as me.
Are you ready Billy?

STAN
I guess.

Grandpa flips the switch on the tape player.
A slow Enya song begins to play.

ENYA
(Singing)
'Take a look, take a look...'

As the song continues, Stan is forced to just sit in the dark room and listen to it.

Finally, Stan grabs the doorknob, but it's locked.

STAN
Okay, you can let me out now.

GRANDPA
Not just yet.

Grandpa turns the song up louder.
Stan pulls on the door.

STAN
LET ME OUT, GRANDPA!!

The song gets even louder still.

STAN
I can't take it anymore! This music is terrible!! It's cheesy but lame and eerily soothing at the same time!!

GRANDPA
THAT'S IT!!!!
NOW YOU KNOW WHAT IT FEELS LIKE TO BE GRANDPA!!!!

EXT. STAN'S HOUSE - HALLWAY

Grandpa opens the door.
Stan falls out, looking terrible and beaten.

Grandpa flips off the Enya music, and goes over to Stan.

STAN
Grandpa... I... I had no idea how bad it was for you...
Now I understand...

GRANDPA
So now will you kill me, Billy?

STAN
Sure I will, Grandpa... I will.

EXT. TOON CENTRAL

The people of South Park are still gathered around
Cartoon Central, only now, they have chained
themselves to the building.

STAN'S MOM
It doesn't look like our protest is working.

KYLE'S MOM
It'll work... It has to...

Suddenly, a well-dressed businessman emerges from the
doors of the building.

KYLE'S MOM (cont'd)
Look! It's the president of the network!!

JOHN WARSOG
Ladies and gentlemen, my name is John Warsog. I have
prepared a statement for you on behalf of the network...

The people all stand up. Warsog puts on glasses and pulls
a piece of paper out of his pocket.

He clears his throat, and unfolds the piece of paper.
Finally he begins to read.

JOHN WARSOG (cont'd)
'Fuck you.'

John folds the piece of paper and puts it back into his
pocket. He takes off his glasses.

JOHN WARSOG
Thank you, ladies and gentlemen. If there are any
questions, you may direct them to that brick
wall over there.

SOUTH PARK (5) PAGE 137

Scene 310 | Panel | BG

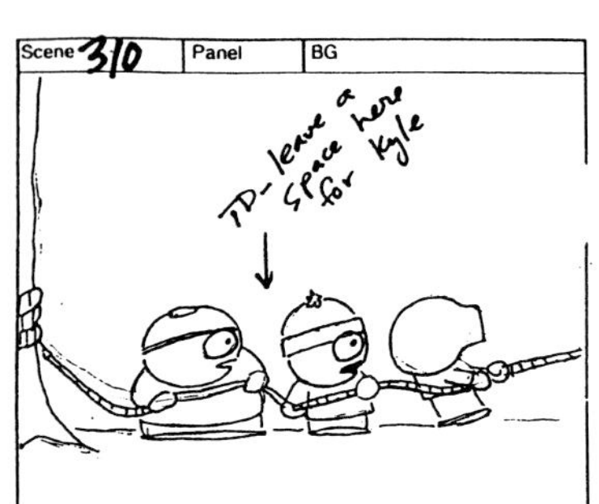

Scene 310 cont. | Panel | BG

Scene 311 | Panel | BG

Location/Time

Dialogue

STAN
Kay, come on, guys.

Action/Efx

Trans.

Location/Time

Dialogue

The boys all grab the rope, and start to hoist the cow up, using a branch above grandpa's head as a pully.

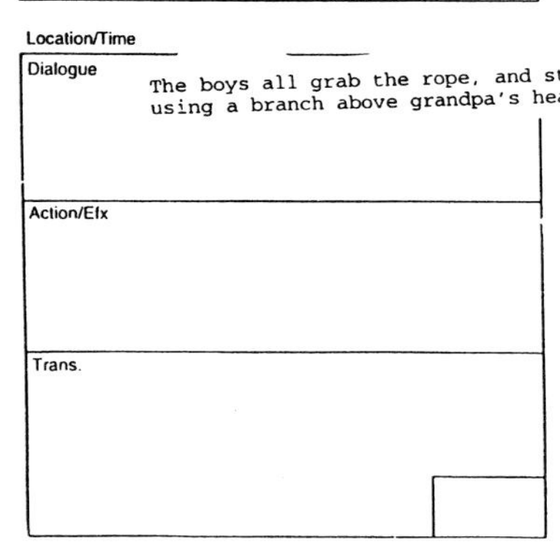

Action/Efx

Trans.

Location/Time

CARTMAN
Why don't we just shoot him?

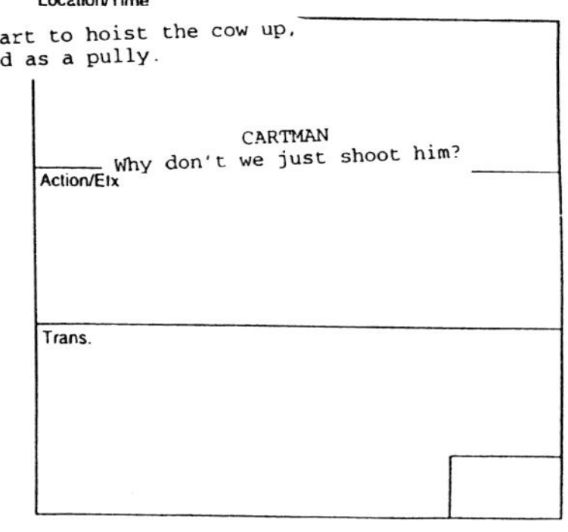

Action/Efx

Trans.

SOUTH PARK (5) PAGE 138

Scene 312 | Panel | BG

Scene 313 | Panel | BG

Scene 314 | Panel | BG

Location/Time

Dialogue

STAN
You dumbass, Cartman! It has to look natural, or else we'll all get busted.

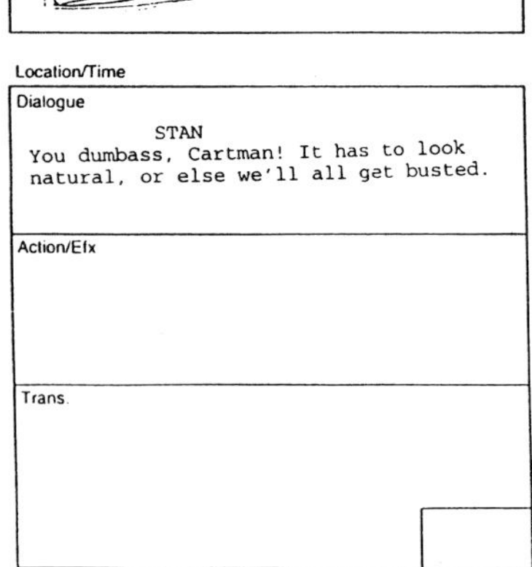

Action/Efx

Trans.

Location/Time

Dialogue

KYLE
Yeah, stupid.

Action/Efx

Trans.

The boys pull on the rope and the cow gets hoisted up over grandpa.

GRANDPA
That's good, Billy... A little higher now...

Action/Efx

Trans.

John walks back into the building.
Kyle's mother is furious.

KYLE'S MOTHER
HEY, YOU WILL NOT GET AWAY WITH THIS!!!

John pauses to pull down his pants and moon the crowd, then continues on into the building.

KYLE'S MOTHER (cont'd)
THAT DOES IT! NO MORE MR. NICE PROTESTORS!
It's time for PLAN B!

CARTMAN'S MOM
Oh Carol, where are the port-o-potties?

KYLE'S MOTHER
Over there hon.
What, you need to drop some friends off at the pool?

CARTMAN'S MOM
Oh yes indeedy!

The two women laugh, in spite of themselves.

Cartman's mom runs to the toilet, slams the door, and shits up a storm.

EXT. FOREST CLEARING - NIGHT

Grandpa is sitting below a large tree.

STAN
Okay, Grandpa, all you have to do is sit there.
We'll do the rest. You got the cow all tied up?

Kyle finishes putting a rope around a scared cow's waist.

KYLE
Yep, all done.

STAN
Okay, come on, guys.

The boys all grab the rope, and start to hoist the cow up, using a branch above grandpa's head as a pulley.

CARTMAN
Why don't we just shoot him?

STAN
You dumbass, Cartman! It has to look natural,
or else we'll all get busted.

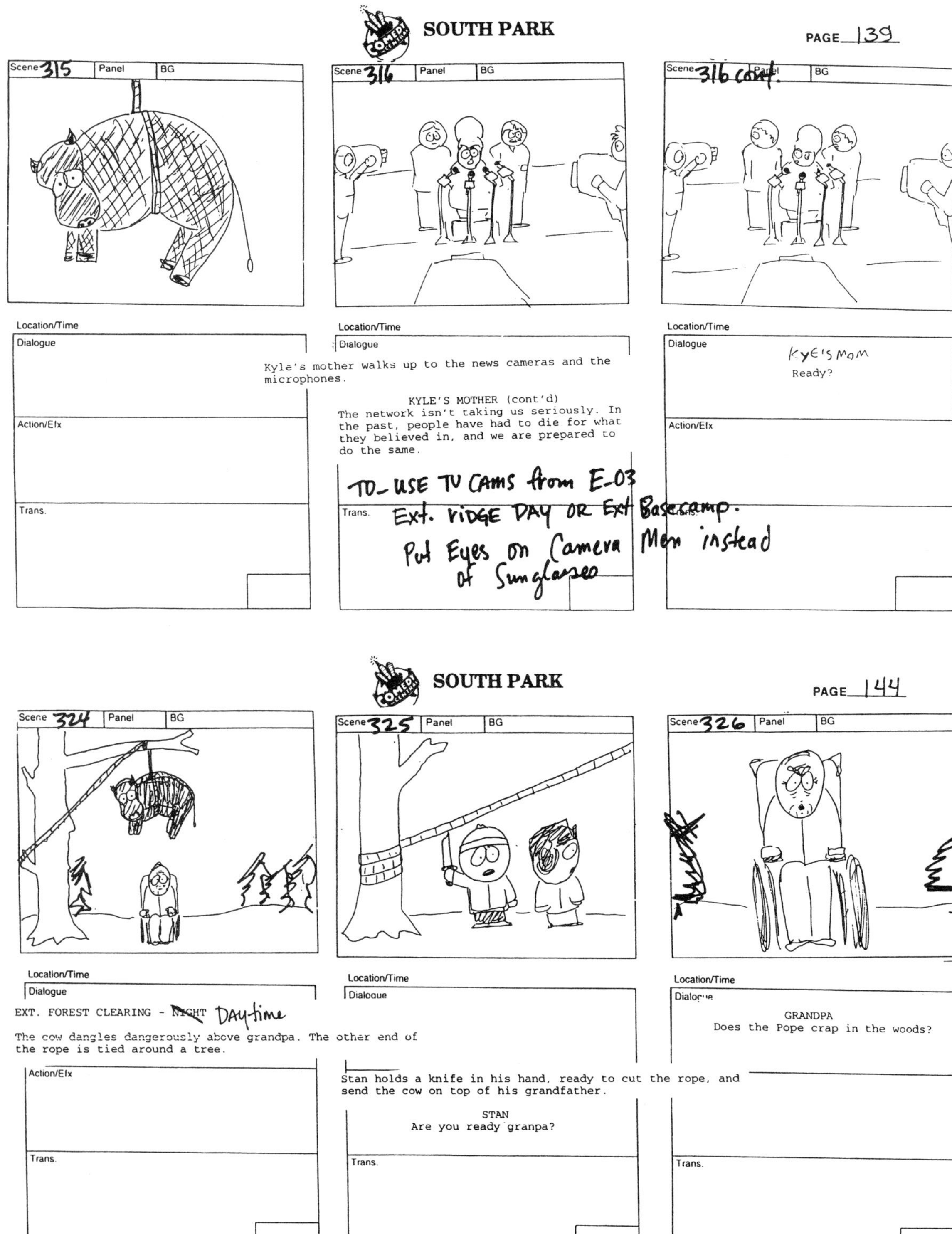

SOUTH PARK
PAGE 139
Scene 315
Panel
BG
Scene 316
Panel
BG
Scene 316 cont.
Panel
BG
Location/Time
Dialogue
Action/Efx
Trans.
Kyle's mother walks up to the news cameras and the microphones.
KYLE'S MOTHER (cont'd)
The network isn't taking us seriously. In the past, people have had to die for what they believed in, and we are prepared to do the same.
TO- USE TV CAMS from E-03
Ext. RIDGE DAY OR Ext Basecamp.
Put Eyes on Camera Men instead of Sunglasses
KYE'S MOM
Ready?
SOUTH PARK
PAGE 144
Scene 324
Scene 325
Scene 326
EXT. FOREST CLEARING - NIGHT Day-time
The cow dangles dangerously above grandpa. The other end of the rope is tied around a tree.
Stan holds a knife in his hand, ready to cut the rope, and send the cow on top of his grandfather.
STAN
Are you ready granpa?
GRANDPA
Does the Pope crap in the woods?

KYLE
Yeah, stupid.

The boys pull on the rope and the cow gets hoisted up over Grandpa.

GRANDPA
That's good, Billy... A little higher now...

The cow dangles in the air. The boys wrap their end of the rope around the base of another tree.

EXT. TOON CENTRAL - NIGHT

Kyle's mother walks up to the news cameras and the microphones.

KYLE'S MOTHER (cont'd)
The network isn't taking us seriously. In the past, people have had to die for what they believed in, and we are prepared to do the same. Ready?

The people near the sling-shot all nod.

KYLE'S MOTHER
Mr. McKormick, you shall be a martyr to us all. God speed.

KYLE'S MOTHER (cont'd)
WE WILL NOT LET THESE CORPORATE HALF-WITS RUIN OUR CHILDREN'S MINDS!! LAUNCH!!!

The sling-shot is cut, Mr. McKormick goes flying into the air and hits SPLAT!! into the side of the Toon Central building, dying instantly.

The news people all gasp.

KYLE'S MOTHER (cont'd)
We will all follow suit!
One by one if that's what it takes!!

The line to the port-o-potties is getting longer. People moan with stomach aches.

EXT. FOREST CLEARING - NIGHT

The cow dangles dangerously above Grandpa. The other end of the rope is tied around a tree.

Stan holds a knife in his hand, ready to cut the rope, and send the cow on top of his grandfather.

STAN
Are you ready Grandpa?

SOUTH PARK
PAGE 147
Scene 333
Panel
BG S/A 328
Location/Time
Dialogue
BARBRADY
... Carry on.
Barbrady drives away. The boys all sigh.
Action/Efx
Trans.
Scene 334
Panel
BG
Location/Time
Dialogue
STAN
Okay, here we go... Bye Grandpa, it was nice knowing you.
Action/Efx
Trans.
Scene 335
Panel
BG
Location/Time
Dialogue
GRANDPA
Cut the damn rope already!
Action/Efx
Trans.
SOUTH PARK
PAGE 148
Scene 336
Panel
BG
FLASH
Location/Time
Dialogue
But now another FLASH!! This one is HUGE. The boys all reel back from its glow.
Action/Efx
BG is just Stock Mtn & trees
Add full frame of White
full frame of Black
2 sets of lightning (yellow & Black)
off to Side
Trans.
Scene 337
Panel
BG
Location/Time
Dialogue
KYLE
Woa, what is that?!
Action/Efx
Trans.
Scene 338
Panel
BG S/A 336
Location/Time
Dialogue
Action/Efx
When the smoke clears, the boys see a tall figure, dressed black and carrying a sythe.
Trans
STAN
Woa... It looks like... death!

GRANDPA
Does the Pope crap in the woods?

Stan is about to cut the rope when suddenly, a light flashes!

The boys all look over at the road, where Officer Barbrady has pulled up in his patrol car.

Barbrady studies the scene from his car, he looks at the cow, the grandpa below it, Stan with the knife in his hand...

The boys' eyes all grow wide.

A long time passes.

BARBRADY
... Carry on.

Barbrady drives away. The boys all sigh.

STAN
Okay, here we go... Bye Grandpa, it was nice knowing you.

GRANDPA
Cut the damn rope already!

But now another FLASH!! This one is HUGE. The boys all reel back from its glow.

KYLE
Woa, what is that?!

When the smoke clears, the boys see a tall figure, dressed in black and carrying a scythe.

STAN
Woa... It looks like... Death!

GRANDPA
It's about time you late ass lazy son of a whore!

Death looks down at Grandpa.

GRANDPA
Come on! Let's go!

But Death walks past Grandpa and heads towards the boys.

GRANDPA
What the -

STAN
Hey, he's coming towards US!

CARTMAN
Why is Death coming after us?

But Death relentlessly heads for the boys.
The boys all scream and run.

INT. STAN'S HOUSE

The boys run inside. Death is just behind them.
It makes a horrible sound.

DEATH
Mrrrrr...

The boys all run up into Stan's room and slam
the door shut. Death is just on the other side,
pounding on the door.

THE BOYS
Help, run, run, run!

CARTMAN
What are we gonna do?!

Stan looks over at his telephone.

EXT. TOON CENTRAL - DAY

REPORTER
As the day progresses, more and more South Park
residents continue to sling-shot their bodies into the
side of the Toon Central building.

Behind him, an OLD LADY flies through the air and
splats into the building.

REPORTER
Toon Central is under incredible pressure to cancel
the show, and has already lost over 20 percent
of their sponsors...

Kyle's mother walks up to Stan's mother and
hands her a cell phone.

KYLE'S MOTHER
Here, Carol, I think it's your boy.

STAN'S MOTHER
Oh, thanks.
(Into the phone)
What is it, Stanley hon? Did you break something?

INT. STAN'S HOUSE

STAN
Mom, Death is here and he's trying to take all of us away with him.

The boys all look worriedly at the door which is still pounding and shaking.

EXT. TOON CENTRAL

STAN'S MOTHER
Stanley honey, you need to leave Mommy alone, I'm doing something very, very important for your little well-being there.

STAN
Yeah, but Mom -

STAN'S MOTHER
Here honey, talk to your father.

Stan's dad gets on the phone.

STAN'S FATHER
Did you turn the heat down?

STAN
Dad, Death is coming -

STAN'S FATHER
Keep the thermostat under 70. Take care of your grandfather.

Click.

INT. STAN'S HOUSE

Stan hangs up the phone. Death starts carving away at the door with his sicle.

STAN
Dammit! You know, I think that if parents would spend less time worrying about what their kids watch on T.V. and more time worrying about what's going on in their kids' lives, this world would be a much better place.

KYLE
Yes, I think that parents get only get so offended by television because they rely on it as a babysitter and the sole educator of their kids.

KENNY
Mph rmph rm rmph rm rmph mmm rmph mph mph rmp mm.

KYLE
Totally, dude.

STAN
Good point, man.

Suddenly, Death BURSTS THROUGH THE DOOR!!!

STAN
AAGH!!

KYLE
Quick! Jump out the window!!

Just before Death can reach them, the boys jump out the window.

COMMERCIAL BREAK #3

ACT III

EXT. SOUTH PARK AVENUE - NIGHT

The boys run screaming down South Park Avenue. Death pursues them on a tricycle.

Grandpa is pursuing Death in his wheelchair.

GRANDPA
Come back here you pompass son of a panzy!

Slowly, Death catches up to the boys, he stretches out his bony hand...

STAN
AAGH!!

KYLE
Don't let him touch you! You die if he touches you!!

GRANDPA
I'm over here you son of a whore!

Death chases the boys past a T.V. shop, where dozens of T.V.s are on in the window.

They are all playing 'Terrance and Phillip'.

ANGLE - TELEVISION

Terrance and Phillip are floating through space with little spacesuits on.

PHILLIP
Oh Terrance... What color is the wind?

Death looks intrigued.

TERRANCE
I don't know why don't you check -

Terrance turns his ass towards Phillip and farts.

PHILLIP
OH! YOU FARTED!!

Death laughs loudly. He has to lay down his scythe to hold his stomach.

TERRANCE
Hey, Phillip, you know what my spacesuit smells like?

PHILLIP
No, Terrance, why don't you tell me?

TERRANCE
Well, it smells like... A dirty fart!

They laugh. Death laughs even harder.

STAN
Hey look!

The boys stop running and notice that Death is watching the show.

Everybody gathers around the T.V. and watches, laughing happily together.

EXT. TOON CENTRAL

The reporter is standing out front of the Toon Central building.

REPORTER
Hours have passed and still the die-hard South Park parents are killing themselves in front of the Toon Central building one by one.

Another person splats into the side of the building.

REPORTER (cont'd)
Worse yet, the stomach flu that seems to be going around is... Wait, wait... I'm getting word that John Warsog, the president of the network is going to make a statement!

Warsog again takes the stand, just as another MAN is about to be released from the sling-shot. A look of relief crosses the man's face.

JOHN WARSOG
Ladies and gentlemen, your Nazi-esque tactics of trying to stink us out with your rancid feces... has worked.

The people look confused.
The port-o-potties are indeed backed up.

JOHN WARSOG
Therefore, today we will officially be taking 'Terrance and Phillip' off the network, and replacing it with reruns of 'She's The Sheriff'. Starring Suzanne Summers.

The people all rejoice and cheer.

JOHN WARSOG (cont'd)
Now get away from here and take your diarrheah with you!

The townspeople all cheer and rejoice. The two guys at the sling-shot accidentally let it go, and the man goes flying into the air and splats against the building.

KYLE'S MOTHER
Now at last we can return to normality!

EXT. SOUTH PARK T.V. SHOP - NIGHT

The boys and Death are still happily watching 'Terrance and Phillip'.

TERRANCE
Hey, Phillip.

PHILLIP
Yes, Terrance.

TERRANCE
Is there a penny stuck in my butt?

PHILLIP
I don't know Terrance, let me check...

CARTMAN
Oh, oh. Don't look there Phillip, you're going to get farted on!!

Phillip moves his head towards Terrance's ass when suddenly FWOOP! A second of static and then the Toon Central logo.

The boys and Death look confused.

NARRATOR
We interrupt this program to bring you some loud static.

Loud static fills the screen.

Death goes absolutely bolistic.
It lets out a horrible cry.

DEATH
MARRRR!!!!!

And turns back on the boys.

KYLE
AAGH!!

Death stretches out its skeleton hand and touches Kenny.
Kenny immediately falls to the ground.

KYLE
Oh my God! They killed Kenny!!

The boys stop and look at Kenny's motionless body.

KYLE
(To Death)
You bastard!!

STAN
Wow, I guess Death was just coming after
Kenny the whole time.

Grandpa wheels himself up, panting.

GRANDPA
HEY! You were supposed to kill ME!!

Death shakes its head.

GRANDPA
That's not fair, God dammit!
My grandpa asked me to kill him and I did it!

Death says nothing, but points his
boney finger to a glowing fog.

STAN
Whoa...

In the glowing fog, another, EXTREMELY OLD man appears,
floating above the ground.

OLD, OLD MAN
Billy...

GRANDPA
Grandpa?

OLD, OLD MAN
That's right, Billy.

SOUTH PARK

PAGE 179

Scene 398 | Panel | BG S/A 391

Location/Time

Dialogue

DEATH
MARRRR!!!!!

Action/Efx

Trans.

Death goes absolutely bolistic. It let's out a horrible cry.

Scene 399 | Panel | BG

Location/Time

Dialogue

KYLE
AAGH!!

Action/Efx

Trans.

And turns back on the boys.

Scene 400 | Panel | BG

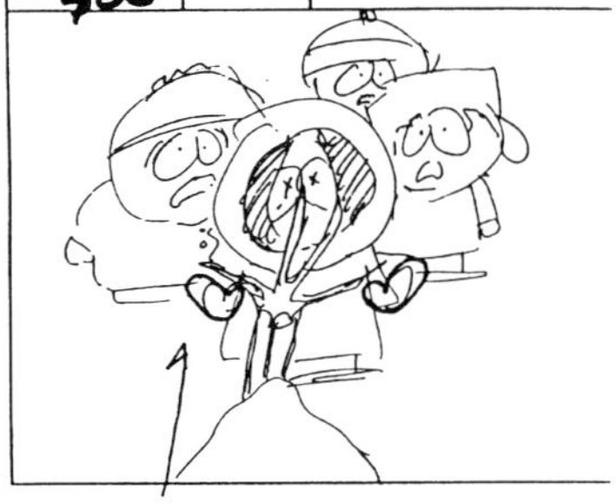

Location/Time

Dialogue

An = Hand should start out of frame

Action/Efx

Death stretches out its skeleton hand and touches Kenny. Kenny immediately falls to the ground.

Trans.

SOUTH PARK

PAGE 180

Scene 401 | Panel | BG

Location/Time

Dialogue

Action/Efx

Trans.

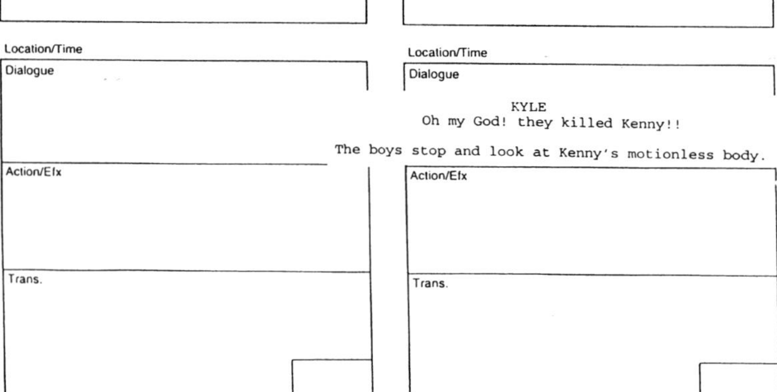

Scene 402 | Panel | BG

Location/Time

Dialogue

KYLE
Oh my God! they killed Kenny!!

The boys stop and look at Kenny's motionless body.

Action/Efx

Trans.

Scene 403 | Panel | BG

Location/Time

Dialogue

KYLE
(To Death)
You bastard!!

Action/Efx

Trans.

GRANDPA
My name's not Billy, Grandpa! And what's wrong with you?
Why do you look all haggard?

OLD, OLD MAN
I asked you to kill me, Billy, but I was wrong...
And now I am forced to spend eternity in limbo.

GRANDPA
Limbo?

OLD, OLD MAN
I was wrong to put you in that position, Billy. Just like you're wrong to put little Billy in it now. You're so obsessed with ending your life, you're not thinking about what you're doing to his.

Grandpa thinks.

OLD, OLD MAN
You must wait to die of natural causes.

GRANDPA
But I've been waiting for twenty-five years! Let nature run its course, or else end up in limbo...

The old, old man starts to fade away.
He, Death and Kenny all float up to the sky.

OLD, OLD MAN (cont'd)
Natural causes, Billy... Natural causes...

STAN
C'mon you guys, let's go home.

Rats come and pull Kenny away.

INT. STAN'S HOUSE - NIGHT

Stan's mom and dad walk in the door.
Kyle's mom is with them.

KYLE'S MOTHER
Here they are!

STAN'S DAD
Well, we did it son! We have fought a battle for your well-being and won!

STAN
What do you mean?

STAN'S MOM
We got 'Terrance and Phillip' taken off the air!

The boys all look terribly disappointed.

CARTMAN
(To Kyle)
You son of a bitch! Your mom sucks!

KYLE'S MOTHER
But look what they put on!

Kyle's mother flips on the television.

TELEVISION
And now back to 'She's the Sheriff'!!

The boys look horribly disappointed.

CARTMAN
NOOOOO!!!! GOD NOOOOOO!!!!!

ANGLE - TELEVISION

SUZANNE SUMMERS
You were the one behind all these shenanigans!

MALE ACTOR
Yeah, well, you're the stupid ho that started it.

KYLE'S MOTHER
What did he say?

SUZANNE SUMMERS
Up yours, buttmunch!

RESUME - LIVING ROOM

The parents are all staring at the T.V.
Kyle's mom is furious.

KYLE'S MOTHER
WHAT-WHAT-WHAAAT?!?!

Kyle's mother picks her sign back up.

KYLE'S MOTHER
Come on everybody! Back to New York!!

The parents all dash out the door.

KYLE
Hey Stan, now that 'Terrance and Phillip' has been taken off the air, what are we going to do for entertainment?

STAN
I dunno... We could start breathing gas fumes...

CARTMAN
My uncle says that smoking crack is kinda cool...

KYLE
Hey! Why don't we go watch some of those
porno movie thingies?

STAN
Cool!

CARTMAN
Yeah!

Grandpa wheels out wearing tourist garb
and holding pamphlets.

STAN
What are you doing, Grandpa?

GRANDPA
I'm planning a trip to Africa. Did you know over 400
people are eaten naturally by lions in Africa every year?

STAN
That's my silly Grandpa!

The boys all laugh and fart.

FIN

EPISODE 113

CARTMAN'S MOM IS A DIRTY SLUT

BY DAVE GOODMAN & TREY PARKER

ACT I

EXT. BUS STOP - DAY

Stan, Kyle and Kenny are waiting for the bus.

STAN
Dude, the bus will be here any minute and Cartman didn't show up for school.

KYLE
Yeah, this is like the third day in a row.
I wonder what's wrong.

KENNY
Mph rmph rm rmph rm.

The boys all laugh.

KYLE
Yeah!

STAN
Hey, maybe we should ditch school and go check on him.

But just then, the school bus pulls up.

MS. CRABTREE
COME ON, WE'RE RUNNING LATE!!!

STAN
We're not getting on, you fat, ugly bitch.

MS. CRABTREE
WHAT DID YOU SAY?!

STAN
I said 'We're not getting on, you fat, ugly bitch.'

MS. CRABTREE
Oh, alright then.

Ms. Crabtree closes the door and drives away.

KYLE
Woa, dude!!

STAN
I always wondered if that would work.

EXT. CARTMAN'S HOUSE

The boys walk up to Cartman's door and knock.
Cartman's mother answers.

MS. CARTMAN
Hello, boys!

KYLE
Hi, we were wondering why Fat Ass - I mean, Cartman - hasn't been showing up for school.

MS. CARTMAN
Oh, he's just been feeling under the weather. Maybe you boys can cheer him up. He's in the back yard.

The boys look at each other suspiciously.

STAN
In the back yard?

EXT. CARTMAN'S BACK YARD

It's a nice little yard. Cartman is sitting at a small, rectangular table covered with a white tablecloth. Cartman is at the head of the table, serving tea with an adorable little plastic tea set. Also seated at the table, are five of Cartman's stuffed animals, one in each chair, and each with a little teacup and saucer in front of them.

CARTMAN
Would you like some more tea, Polly Prissy Pants?

CARTMAN
(Polly voice)
Yes, Eric, I would love some tea, thank you.

CARTMAN
You're very welcome, Polly Prissy Pants.

Unbeknownst to Cartman, the boys sneak in from behind some bushes. They can't believe what they see.

CARTMAN
Would you like some tea, Clyde Frog?

CARTMAN
(Frog voice)
Yes, please. Eric, why are you so cool?

CARTMAN
Oh, I don't know, Clyde Frog, I just am.

CARTMAN
(Polly voice)
You are so strong and smart, Eric. Everybody likes you.

CARTMAN
Why thank you, Polly Prissy Pants, how nice of you.

The boys stay hidden in the bushes.

STAN
Dude, this is pretty fucked up right here.

KENNY
(Laughing)
Mph rm rmph rm rm!

KYLE
Come on! Let's go make fun of him!!

Stan grabs Kyle, stopping him.

STAN
No, dude... This looks really serious.
I think we better get help.

KYLE
Really?

Cartman pours tea for a large, stuffed Panda.

CARTMAN
(Panda voice)
Wow, Eric, you are the coolest guy in the world.
This is tremendous tea!

CARTMAN
Why thank you, Peter Panda. It's a distinctive Earl Grey.

CARTMAN
(Polly voice)
Eric is the best!

CARTMAN
(Frog voice)
Hooray for Eric!

CARTMAN
(Panda voice)
Eric kicks ass!

EXT. COUNSELOR'S OFFICE - DAY

Establishing.

INT. COUNSELOR'S OFFICE - DAY

The boys are gathered around the counselor's desk.
Behind them is a LARGE poster that reads
'FATHER & SON DAY IS COMING'.

KYLE
Mr. Mackey, something's really wrong with Cartman.

SOUTH PARK
PAGE 17 R
Scene 037 Panel BG S/A 035
Location/Time
Dialogue
KYLE
What do you mean?
Action/Efx
Trans.
Scene 038 Panel BG S/A 034
Location/Time
Dialogue
MR. GARRISON
Have you boys noticed anything recently that troubled Eric?
Action/Efx
Trans.
Scene 039 Panel BG S/A 035
Location/Time
Dialogue
STAN
No.
Action/Efx
Trans.
SOUTH PARK
PAGE 18 R
Scene 040 Panel BG S/A 033
FATHER SON PICNIC FRIDAY
Dialogue
*Note- the poster should be very visible in this shot.
MR. GARRISON
Well, obviously something is bothering him.
Trans.
Scene 041 Panel BG S/A 036
Location/Time
Dialogue
Finally Garrison looks up at the wall.
MR. GARRISON
Oh, of course!
Action/Efx
Trans.
Scene 042 Panel BG S/A 035
Location/Time
Dialogue
Action/Efx
Trans.

COUNSELOR
Oh, well there's a newsflash.

STAN
No, no. We saw him having a tea party with his stuffed animals.

KYLE
Yeah, he was doing their voices and pouring tea for them.

COUNSELOR
Oh, okay... Eric is obviously suffering from some kind of emotional distress, okay?

KYLE
What do you mean?

COUNSELOR
Have you boys noticed anything recently that troubled Eric?

STAN
No.

*Note - the poster should be very visible in this shot.

COUNSELOR
Well, obviously something is bothering him, okay?

Finally the counselor looks up at the wall.

COUNSELOR
Oh, of course!

The counselor walks over, right in front of the poster, then reaches past it and grabs a video camera.

COUNSELOR (cont'd)
My video camera! Boys, if you could videotape Eric's behavior, then I can study him psychologically and find out what's wrong, okay?

STAN
Is that legal?

COUNSELOR
Oh, hell yes.

EXT. CARTMAN'S BACK YARD

Cartman is sitting at his cute little table.

CARTMAN
My goodness that's a lovely dress you are wearing, Polly Prissy Pants.

SOUTH PARK PAGE 21

Scene 049 Panel BG S/A 017

Scene 050 Panel BG

Scene 051 Panel BG S/A 047 center on Cartman

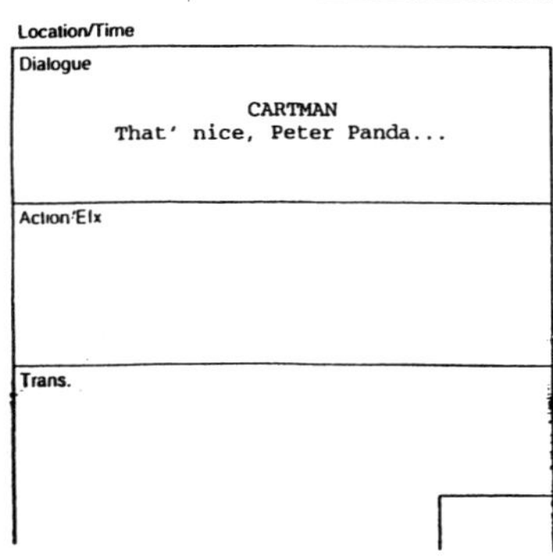

Location/Time

Dialogue

CARTMAN
That' nice, Peter Panda...

Action/Efx

Trans.

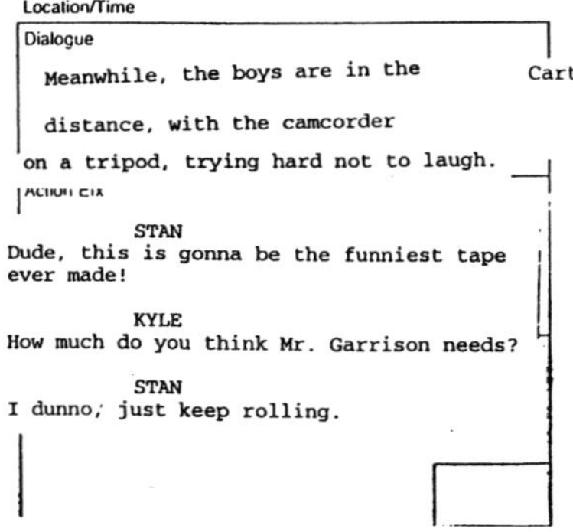

Location/Time

Dialogue

Meanwhile, the boys are in the distance, with the camcorder on a tripod, trying hard not to laugh.

Action/Efx

STAN
Dude, this is gonna be the funniest tape ever made!

KYLE
How much do you think Mr. Garrison needs?

STAN
I dunno, just keep rolling.

Trans.

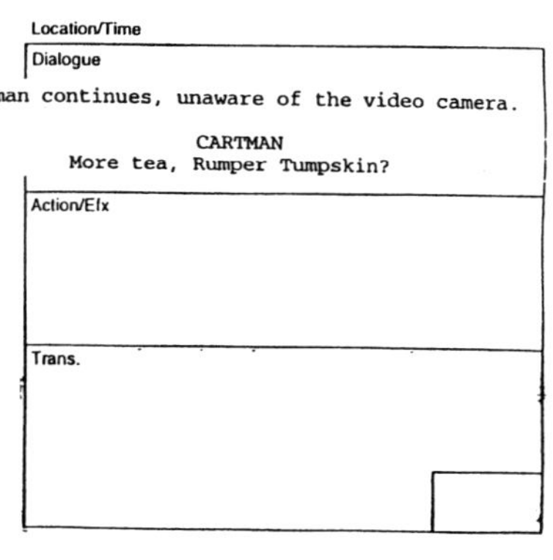

Location/Time

Dialogue

Cartman continues, unaware of the video camera.

CARTMAN
More tea, Rumper Tumpskin?

Action/Efx

Trans.

SOUTH PARK PAGE 22

Scene 052 Panel BG

Location/Time

Dialogue

CARTMAN
(Tumpskin voice)
Yes, please, Eric. You are tough and handsome.

Action/Efx

Trans.

Scene 053 Panel BG S/A 051

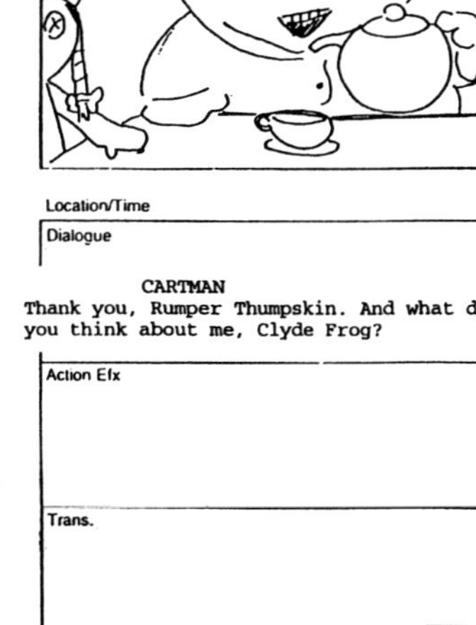

Location/Time

Dialogue

CARTMAN
Thank you, Rumper Thumpskin. And what do you think about me, Clyde Frog?

Action/Efx

Trans.

Scene 054 Panel BG S/A 023

Location/Time

Dialogue

CARTMAN
(Frog voice)
I think you're a big, fat piece of crap.

Action/Efx

Trans.

CARTMAN
(Polly voice)
Oh, thank you, Eric, you are a perfect gentleman. And you are smart and cool.

CARTMAN
(Panda voice)
Yes, Eric, you are strong and smart and cool. Everybody likes you very much.

CARTMAN
That's nice, Peter Panda...

Meanwhile, the boys are in the distance, with the camcorder on a tripod, trying hard not to laugh.

STAN
Dude, this is gonna be the funniest tape ever made!

KYLE
How much do you think Mr. Mackey needs?

STAN
I dunno, just keep rolling.

Cartman continues, unaware of the video camera.

CARTMAN
More tea, Rumper Tumpskin?

CARTMAN
(Tumpskin voice)
Yes, please, Eric. You are tough and handsome.

CARTMAN
Thank you, Rumper Tumpskin. And what do you think about me, Clyde Frog?

CARTMAN
(Frog voice)
I think you're a big, fat piece of crap.

Cartman thinks for a minute.

CARTMAN
HEY!!!

EXT. CARTMAN'S HOUSE - NIGHT

The sun goes down in South Park. Passage of time.

INT. CARTMAN'S HOUSE

Cartman and his mom are sitting at the dinner table. Kitty walks up and meows.

CARTMAN
No, Kitty this is MY corned beef cabbage.

KITTY
Meow.

CARTMAN
No, Kitty!! That's a BAD KITTY!!!

Kitty hisses.

MS. CARTMAN
How is your beefy roast, snookums?

CARTMAN
Mom... Can I ask you a question?

MS. CARTMAN
Sure, hon.

CARTMAN
You know how my friend Stan has, like, a DAD?

MS. CARTMAN
Uh-huh.

CARTMAN
And my friend Kyle has a DAD...
And my friend Kenny has a DAD?

MS. CARTMAN
Yes...

The two just sit there in silence for a LONG TIME.

MS. CARTMAN (cont'd)
Well what's your question, hon?

CARTMAN
(Pissed)
GOD DAMMIT!! Do I have a dad?!?!

MS. CARTMAN
Oh...

CARTMAN
I wanna know where I came from.

MS. CARTMAN
Oh... Hmmm... Well, you see, Eric, sometimes when a man and a woman are attracted to each other, they want to be... CLOSE to each other.

CARTMAN
Uh-huh...

MS. CARTMAN
And, sometimes, the man puts his Hoo-Hoo Dilly in the woman's Cha-Cha.

Cartman tries to understand.

CARTMAN
So, WHO put his Hoo-Hoo Dilly in your Cha-Cha?

Cartman's mother thinks.

MS. CARTMAN
Eric, the day I met your father, it was like magic... It was a beautiful autumn night, when the aspen trees were turning; at the twelfth annual drunken barn dance...

EXT. LARGE BARN - NIGHT - 8 YEARS AGO

A large barn with a banner that reads 'Twelfth Annual Drunken Barn Dance'. From inside, music, screaming, laughing and crashing can be heard.

INT. LARGE BARN - NIGHT

Inside the barn is absolute chaos. People are singing, dancing, fighting... but most of all, drinking. Beer flows from huge steins, steel kegs, and glass bottles. Everyone is absolutely bombed.

MS. CARTMAN (V.O.)
I was young and naive then...

Now we see the younger Ms. Cartman. She looks pretty much the same except that her hair is longer. She is chugging a yard of beer.

MAN
Wow! I've never seen a woman drink that much!! You're amazing, Ms. Cartman!!

MS. CARTMAN
(totally drunk)
Oh, heck, I haven't even started yet! I baked cookies would anybody like one?

OFFICER BARBRADY
I wouldn't mind gettin' a hold of YOUR cookies, Ms. Cartman!

MS. CARTMAN
(Sexy)
Well... Go right ahead, Officer Barbrady...

Barbrady leans into Ms. Cartman... Then grabs a cookie, bites into it and walks away.

OFFICER BARBRADY
Mmm, that's a good cookie!

Square dancing MUSIC kicks in.

JIMBO
Come on everybody, let's do the drunken barn dance!!

Ms. Cartman stumbles over to the dance floor.

MS. CARTMAN (V.O.)
And then I saw him... He was the most beautiful, charming piece of ass I'd ever seen in South Park.

The camera settles on Jimbo for a moment... Was Jimbo Cartman's dad?! No, just then, the crowd parts, and standing there... Is a large, buff Native-American Ute man. He and Ms. Cartman stare at each other.

MS. CARTMAN (V.O.)
His name was Chief Running Water.

As the camera ZOOMS IN on their faces, that gay 'Near/Far' song from 'Titanic' plays.

Ms. Cartman walks over to the Chief and starts to mosh with him, vulgarly.

Finally, Ms. Cartman trips, falls down, gets back up, vomits, and keeps dancing.

INT. CARTMAN'S HOUSE - PRESENT DAY

Cartman is sitting, listening to the story.

MS. CARTMAN
I don't recall exactly how the rest of the night went, but the next morning, I was pregnant with you, my little blueberry muffin.

CARTMAN
So where is Chief Running Water - I mean, DAD, now?

MS. CARTMAN
Oh, I never saw him after that.
I wasn't really that interested in him.

Cartman sits there and thinks for a moment.

CARTMAN
That isn't a very romantic story, Mom!

Ms. Cartman goes back to eating.

MS. CARTMAN
I heard he still lives on the Ute reservation just outside of town.

CARTMAN
Wow... To think all this time I'm actually a Native American.

Kitty walks up and meows.

CARTMAN
NO KITTY! That's a BAD KITTY!!!

EXT. STAN'S HOUSE - ESTABLISHING

INT. STAN'S HOUSE

Stan, Kyle and Kenny are on the couch watching television. Grandpa is watching the T.V. too, but he has the remote control.

ANGLE - T.V.

NARRATOR
Coming this Sunday... A major television event that will blow you away.

Explosions on the T.V. screen. The boys perk up.

NARRATOR
Terrance...

Zoom in on Terrance's face.

NARRATOR
Phillip...

Zoom in on Phillip's face.

NARRATOR
In the harrowing made-for-T.V. drama, 'Not Without My Anus'. Based on a true story.

TERRANCE
Hey Phillip, I have to go to Iraq and find my kidnapped daughter!

PHILLIP
Then I'm going to go with you, Terrance!

Phillip farts, they both laugh merrily.

NARRATOR
See Canada's hottest stars in the HBC movie of the week.

STAN
Wow! Kick ass, dude! We have to remember to tape 'Not Without My Anus' next week.

KYLE
Yeah, dude, it looks riveting.

STAN
C'mon grandpa! We wanna watch 'Terrance and Phillip'!

GRANDPA
No, Billy, we're gonna watch the Bob Saget show.

The boys MOAN.

ANGLE - T.V.

NARRATOR
And now back to 'America's Stupidest Home Videos'. Here's your host, Bob Saget!!!

A clean-shaven Bob Saget takes the stage.

BOB SAGET
Hey, I just flew into the studio, boy are my arms tired.

The audience doesn't react, but Grandpa laughs.

BOB SAGET
Why didn't the skeleton cross the road? 'Cause he didn't have the guts.

The audience again remains silent. Grandpa slaps his knee, laughing. The boys just sit there.

BOB SAGET
Knock, Knock.

BOB SAGET
Bob.

BOB SAGET
Bob Saget.

The audience is stumped for a moment. Silence... Suddenly they ERUPT with laughter. They roll around on the floor, laughing uncontrollably. So is Grandpa. Stan can't believe it.

STAN
This guy sucks!

KYLE
Yeah, he's almost as bad as that guy on 'Full House'.

Suddenly, the doorbell rings. The boys walk over to answer it. When Stan opens the door, he finds Cartman dressed all in Indian garb.

STAN
Cartman? What the hell are you doing dressed up like an Indian with a bear necklace?

CARTMAN
Native American, Stan. And the bear is very important to my people.

STAN
What?

Kyle and Kenny walk up behind Stan and check Cartman out. Kenny immediately starts laughing uncontrollably.

CARTMAN
HEY! THE WHITE MAN HAS MOCKED MY PEOPLE LONG ENOUGH! YOU KEEP YOUR GOD DAMNED MOUTH SHUT!!!
(Back to normal)
Stan, I need to borrow your bike to ride over to the reservation.

STAN
What are you talking about, Cartman?

CARTMAN
My name isn't Eric Cartman. It's Eric Running Water. Now, can I borrow your bike, or do I have to kick you in the nuts and steal it?

STAN
Go ahead, dude.

Cartman leaves, closing the door behind him. The boys head back to the couch.

KYLE
Man, Cartman's more screwed up than I thought.

STAN
(holding out VHS tape)
Yeah, we better get this video tape over to Mr. Mackey quick.

ANGLE - T.V.

BOB SAGET (cont'd)
Just a friendly reminder to all of you out there, send us your stupidest home videos! The grand prize this month will be ten thousand dollars!!

GRANDPA
Ten thousand dollars!! Holy smokes!!

KYLE
Wow! I wish WE had a stupidest home video!

Suddenly, the boys all seem to get the same idea.
The camera PANS along each kid's face as MUSIC kicks in.
They look at their tape with wide eyes.

EXT. UTE INDIAN RESERVATION - DAY

A NATIVE AMERICAN man walks up to a campfire,
where several other Utes are sitting.

CHIEF RUNNING WATER
... And Bear cried to Eagle...

NATIVE AMERICAN
Running Water, there's some kid here to see you.

CHIEF RUNNING WATER
What kid?

NATIVE AMERICAN
He claims to be YOUR kid.

Just then, Cartman walks up, wearing
all kinds of Indian garb.

CARTMAN
Hi, Dad!

CHIEF RUNNING WATER
Who the hell are you?

CARTMAN
I'm your son, Eric. My mom says you put your Hoo-Hoo Dilly
in her Cha-Cha at the drunken barn dance.

CHIEF RUNNING WATER
Your mother?

CARTMAN
Liane Cartman.

CHIEF RUNNING WATER
CARTMAN?!
(Laughing) Oh, boy I was worried there for a second!!
Look, kid, I'm not your father.

CARTMAN
But my mom said YOU were the guy she was with.

CHIEF RUNNING WATER
Kid, I hate to break this to you, but your mother is what we Native Americans refer to as 'Bear with wide canyon'.

CARTMAN
What do you mean?

CHIEF RUNNING WATER
She is 'Doe who cannot keep legs together'.

CARTMAN
Huh?

CHIEF RUNNING WATER
Your mom's a slut.

CARTMAN
HEY!

CHIEF RUNNING WATER
Don't feel too bad, your mom was just too drunk to remember what happened. Let me tell you...

EXT. LARGE BARN - NIGHT

We are again outside the drunken barn dance.

INT. LARGE BARN - NIGHT

The younger Chief Running Water and Ms. Cartman laugh and dance into the hay loft, a few yards away from the party.

Ms. Cartman giggles as she and the Chief fall into the hay, embracing each other.

They look into each other's eyes for a beat...

CHIEF RUNNING WATER
We got tired of dancing, so we went off to find a private spot. I knew that she wanted me because she kept saying romantic things.

MS. CARTMAN
Oh Chief, I want your hot manchowder.

CHIEF RUNNING WATER
Woa! Hello!

The two start going at it, as random townspeople dance and vomit past them.

MS. CARTMAN
Wait, wait!!

Ms. Cartman sits up.

MS. CARTMAN
Who is THAT?!

Again the crowd parts, and this time we see a younger CHEF standing in the crowd with a big afro. Again, the 'Near/Far' faggot song from 'Titanic' plays as the camera zooms in on Ms. Cartman's and Chef's faces.

MS. CARTMAN
Chief... Could you excuse me for a minute?

CHIEF RUNNING WATER
Huh?

Ms. Cartman gets up and walks over to Chef.

CHIEF RUNNING WATER (cont'd)
You gotta be kidding me!!

MS. CARTMAN
Why, hello there... I don't think I've seen you around before.

CHEF
Naw, I'm new in town.

MS. CARTMAN
Well, what's a nice, handsome,
(looking down)
BLACK... man like yourself doing in a pit like South Park?

CHEF
I'm gonna open up my own restaurant here!

MS. CARTMAN
My, how exciting! Would you...
Care to put your tongue in my mouth?

CHEF
Damn, baby, you cut right to the chase, don't you?

MS. CARTMAN
I'm plastered.

Ms. Cartman grabs Chef and starts violently French kissing him.

EXT. UTE INDIAN RESERVATION - PRESENT DAY

CARTMAN
His TONGUE?! CHEF?! Chef is my dad?!

CHIEF RUNNING WATER
He's the last person I saw with your mom that night.

CARTMAN
Oh my God! I'm a black African American!!

ACT II

EXT. BUS STOP - DAY

Stan, Kyle and Kenny are hanging out at the bus stop with a little go-cart.

Kenny is pulling at the lawnmower type engine, trying to get it to start.

STAN
Come on, Kenny. Get the go-cart going. I wanna ride it!!

KYLE
Did you send the videotape to 'America's Stupidest Home Videos'?

STAN
Yeah, I mailed it last night. What sucks is that now we'll have to actually watch that Bob Saget guy to find out if we won.

KYLE
If we win, we can buy a NEW go-cart that actually RUNS!

STAN
Shh! Here comes Cartman!

Cartman walks up, wearing all kinds of black hip hop street garb and sporting a large afro.

CARTMAN
Ssup, homies?

STAN
Cartman?

CARTMAN
I was just down in the SPC kicking it with some G's on the west side.

KYLE
You live on the EAST side, Cartman!

STAN
Dude, I thought you said you were Native American.

CARTMAN
Oh, right. Like I'm some hippy Indian!

SOUTH PARK
PAGE 105
Scene 220 cont.
Panel
BG
Location/Time
Dialogue
to check for blood. He appears okay.
Action/Efx
Trans.
Scene 221
Panel
BG
Location/Time OUTSKIRTS REV
Dialogue
Action/Efx
Trans.
Scene 222
Panel
BG
Location/Time Rev
Dialogue
Action/Efx
Trans.
SOUTH PARK
PAGE 106
Scene 223
Panel
BG S/A 220
Location/Time SP OUTSKIRTS
Dialogue
Action/Efx
Trans.
Scene 223 cont.
Panel
BG
Location/Time
Dialogue
Until a train runs him over going seventy.
Action/Efx
Trans.
Scene 224
Panel
BG
Location/Time
Dialogue
Action/Efx
Trans.

CARTMAN (cont)
You know what I'm sayin'? Check you later, I'm gonna go chill with my dad.

Cartman walks off.

STAN
Dude, we should be videotaping THIS! We could make ANOTHER ten thousand dollars!

Just then, Kenny manages to get the go-cart running. It takes off at an amazing speed! Kenny is dragged behind it, holding desperately onto the cord.

STAN AND KYLE
HOLD ON KENNY!!!

The go-cart runs wild up and down the street, though the trees, Kenny being dragged and beaten to a bloody pulp. Finally, after horrible bounces and bumps, the go-cart comes to a stop. Kenny manages to slowly sit up. He waves to Stan and Kyle. He appears okay.

KENNY
Mrph mfrr mphr.

Until a train runs him over going seventy.

STAN
Oh my God!! They've killed Kenny!!

KYLE
YOU BASTARDS!!!

EXT. CHEF'S HOUSE - DAY

Cartman knocks on the door. Chef answers.

CHEF
Hello?

CARTMAN
Yo, pops.

Cartman is standing there with his afro.

CHEF
Boy, what the fudge are you doing?!

CARTMAN
You know, just laying down some rhymes for my G-folk. You know what I'm saying?

CHEF
Get in here!

CARTMAN
West side!

Chef grabs Cartman by the arm and yanks him into his house.

INT. CHEF'S HOUSE - DAY

CHEF
(Grabbing the afro)
Take off that wig!! Now what's gotten into you?

CARTMAN
YOU'RE my dad, Chef! Chief Running Water said you got together with my mom at the drunken barn dance.

CHEF
What? No...
(Thinking to himself)
Uh... Did I?

CARTMAN
He said you kissed her with your tongue.

CHEF
Oh! Oh, that's different! Women don't get pregnant from tongue kissing, children!

Cartman just stands there, blinking.

CARTMAN
(Looking sad)
So, you're not my dad?

CHEF
Of course not. Here,
(Helping Cartman onto a stool)
you children sit down and let me explain something to you about where babies come from. Then you'll see why I can't be your dad.

Music kicks in. Chef gets ready to sing.

CHEF
(Singing)
When a man loves a woman and a woman loves a man
(actually, sometimes the man doesn't love
the woman, but he acts like he does in
order to get some action)
the magic starts to happen and the two
take off their clothes - that's right.
They caress and touch each other until a
part of the man grows.
Oooh, they roll around and now things are
really starting to get hot.

And the man say, "I love you" and the woman says, "Hold on a second, I gotta go to the bathroom."
So you wait and you wait and you wait and you wait and. . .
You wait and you wait and you wait.
You wait and you're cooling down and she's still going to the bathroom.
Finally she comes back and she says, "Baby I'm getting hot."
And that's when you gotta jump her butt and pump her full of...

Cartman is tremendously confused.

CARTMAN
WHAT?! So who the hell did that to my mom at the drunken barn dance?!?!

Chef thinks.

CHEF
Oh, children, that was a long time ago...
But I'll tell you what I remember...

EXT. LARGE BARN - NIGHT

Same old establishing shot. Loud noises and music inside.

INT. LARGE BARN - NIGHT

Chef and Ms. Cartman are rolling around in the hay, with their tongues in each other's mouths. Ms. Cartman is on her back, Chef is on top of her.

MS. CARTMAN
Oh, Chef! You're so strong!!

JIMBO
Hey everybody! Look who's here!!
The AFC champion Denver Broncos!!!

Sure enough the entire Denver Bronco team walks in.

BRONCOS
(Ad libbing)
Are we too late for the party? Where's the beer? etc.

Ms. Cartman, still on top of Chef, turns to look at the Denver Broncos.

Once again, the gay 'Near/Far' 'Titanic' song starts, this time the camera ZOOMS in on Ms. Cartman's face and then ZOOMS in on the entire 1991 Denver Broncos team.

MS. CARTMAN
Oh, Chef! OH, CHEF!!

Chef looks surprised.

CHEF
Damn woman, what's gotten into to you?

MS. CARTMAN
WHOOPEE!!!

Suddenly, a hand emerges from beneath Ms. Cartman. Chef pulls the hay away to reveal... MR. GARRISON!!

CHEF
Garrison!! What the hell are you doing?!

Garrison looks at his hand.

MR. GARRISON
You're DRUNK, Mr. HAT!!

As Ms. Cartman looks at Garrison, that gay 'Near/Far' song from 'Titanic' swells up yet again. ZOOM IN on Ms. Cartman's and Garrison's faces.

CHEF
Ah, MAN!! I'm outta here!

MS. CARTMAN
Come on, Chef. Haven't you ever heard of a 'manage' au three'?

CHEF
Yeah, when two women are involved!

Chef gets up and leaves.

MR. GARRISON
Damn! Damn, Damn! Oh well, guess it'll just have to be you and me, Ms. Cartman.

They roll around in the hay.

INT. CHEF'S HOUSE - DAY

CHEF
And THAT'S who she was with last... Mr. Garrison.

CARTMAN
No! NOOOO!!!! NO GOD NO!!!!!!

INT. STAN'S HOUSE - NIGHT

ANGLE - T.V.

ANNOUNCER
And now back to 'America's Stupidest Home Videos'.

BOB SAGET
Here's a video sent to us, that shows a
VERY disturbed little boy...

ANGLE - VIDEO SCREEN

A clip of what Kyle filmed of Cartman. No voice-over. Just Cartman's insanity.

CARTMAN
(on the monitor)
'Why thank you Polly Prissy Pants,
you are my best friend.'

The audience begins to laugh.

CARTMAN
(on the monitor/as Polly)
'I think you are one of the coolest people in the world
Eric, and you are not fat at all!'

CARTMAN
'Really? You don't think so?'

CARTMAN
(on the monitor/as Clyde frog)
'No you're not fat.'

The audience goes apeshit. They are hysterical.

ANGLE - KIDS

Stan and Kyle are laughing. Just then, Stan's mother and father walk in.

STAN'S MOTHER
Oh, Stanley, we just heard the news that your little
friend Kenny was killed by a train this morning.

STAN
Huh? Oh, yeah.

STAN'S FATHER
Is there anything we can do for you, son?

Stan thinks.

STAN
How about some ice cream!

KYLE
Yeah! With butterscotch!

STAN'S MOTHER
You bet... You poor dears.

Stan's father and mother walk out.

ANGLE - T.V.

BOB SAGET
Now the moment you've all been waiting for, when one of our lucky videos qualifies for the TEN-THOUSAND-DOLLAR grand prize to be chosen TOMORROW NIGHT. The winner is:
(Drumroll)
Little Boy's Tea Party!

ANGLE - KIDS

The boys go absolutely wild, jumping and hollering. Clapping is heard from the T.V.

BOYS
(Ad lib)
Yeah! Wooo! I knew we'd win!

STAN
We're in the finals!

KYLE
We're going to win ten thousand dollars!

STAN
Man, Cartman's going to be famous.

INT. SOUTH PARK BAR - NIGHT

Garrison is drinking at the local bar with most of the townspeople of South Park.

MR. GARRISON
Well, I guess we should go, Mr. Hat...

MR. HAT
Oh, just one more Cosmopolitan, Mr. Garrison.

MR. GARRISON
Mr. Hat, you need to admit you have a drinking problem...
Another Cosmo please!

Just then, Cartman slams the door open. He's standing in the doorway, eyes fixed on Garrison, looking pissed off.

CARTMAN
All this time... Why didn't you tell me, father?

MR. GARRISON
What the hell are you talking about, Eric?

CARTMAN
It was YOU all along!!

Garrison doesn't answer... Perhaps he IS Eric's father!

CARTMAN
YOU were with my mother the night of the drunken barn dance!

JIMBO
Garrison?! That's impossible! He's gay!

MR. GARRISON
I am NOT GAY!!

CARTMAN
Then you DID sleep with my mom?

MR. GARRISON
No!

JIMBO
He's gay!

Garrison thinks. He doesn't know what to say.

MR. GARRISON
Okay, okay! I admit it!! I might have made love to your mother at the drunken barn dance!!

Cartman's face lights up.

MR. GARRISON
But who here DIDN'T?!?!

The room is silent.

MR. GARRISON
Now come on! Honestly, who has NEVER had sex with Mrs. Cartman?

Everybody looks to one another. Nobody speaks up... Not even the preacher or Jesus.

MAN
I haven't!

MR. GARRISON
You don't count, halfie! You don't have any legs!

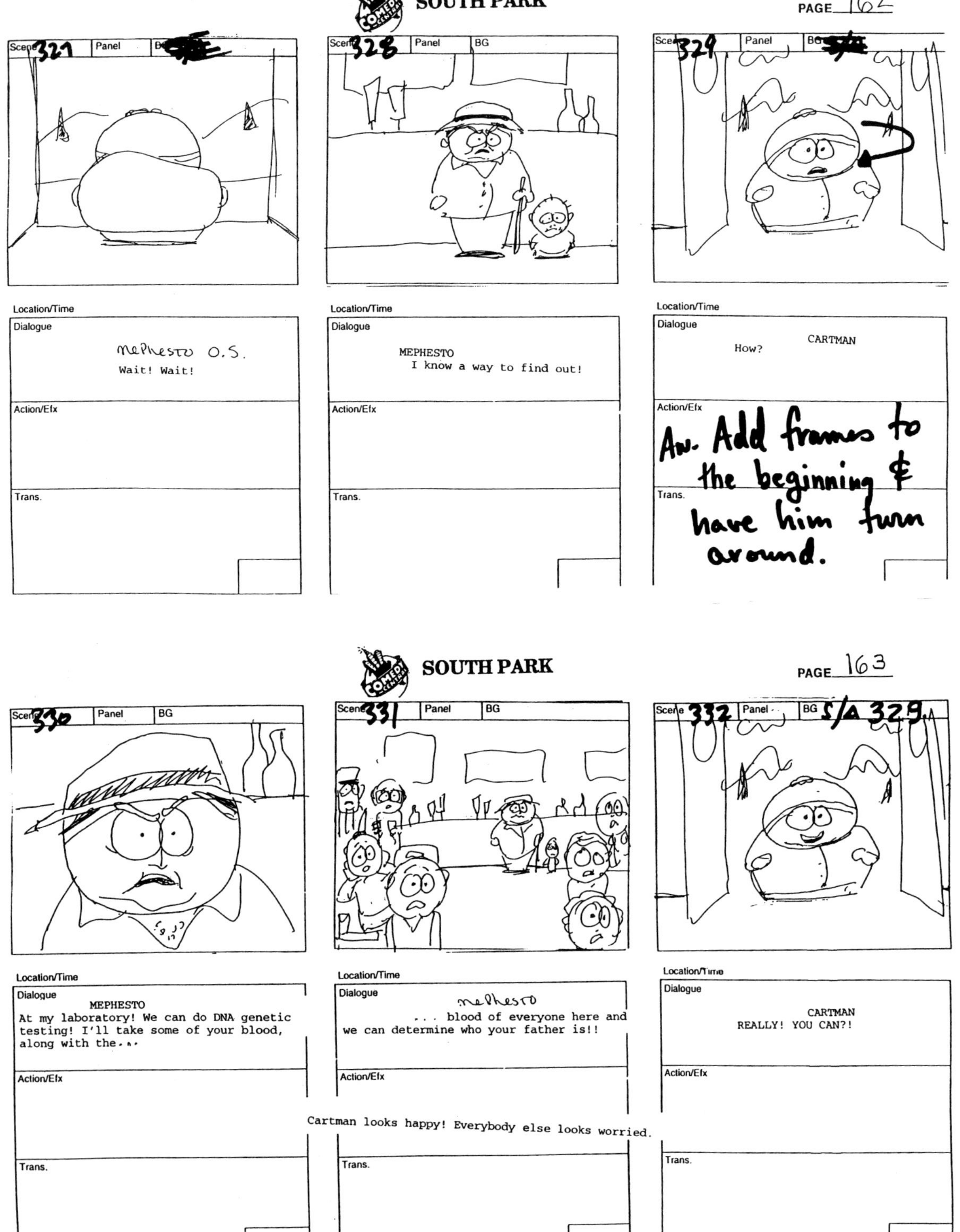
SOUTH PARK
PAGE 162
Scene 327 Panel BG
Scene 328 Panel BG
Scene 329 Panel BG
Location/Time
Dialogue
mePhesto O.S.
Wait! Wait!
Action/Efx
Trans.
Location/Time
Dialogue
MEPHESTO
I know a way to find out!
Action/Efx
Trans.
Location/Time
Dialogue
CARTMAN
How?
Action/Efx
An. Add frames to the beginning & have him turn around.
Trans.
SOUTH PARK
PAGE 163
Scene 330 Panel BG
Scene 331 Panel BG
Scene 332 Panel BG S/A 329
Location/Time
Dialogue
MEPHESTO
At my laboratory! We can do DNA genetic testing! I'll take some of your blood, along with the...
Action/Efx
Trans.
Location/Time
Dialogue
mePhesto
... blood of everyone here and we can determine who your father is!!
Action/Efx
Cartman looks happy! Everybody else looks worried.
Trans.
Location/Time
Dialogue
CARTMAN
REALLY! YOU CAN?!
Action/Efx
Trans.

MAN
Oh, yeah.

Cartman can't believe it.

MR. GARRISON
So you see, Eric. Anyone here could be your father.
I'm afraid you're never going to know...

Cartman puts his head down.

JIMBO
Don't feel too bad there, kid. I never knew
who my father was either...
(Pause)
I mean, I DID know who he was, and, well, we had great
times together and huntin' and fishin', but - well,
hell, you know what I mean.

Cartman slowly walks out of the bar. Very sad violin
music begins to play. Everyone looks like they
genuinely feel bad for Eric.

MEPHESTO
Wait! Wait! I know a way to find out!

CARTMAN
How?

MEPHESTO
At my laboratory! We can do DNA genetic testing! I'll take
some of your blood, along with the blood of everyone here
and we can determine who your father is!!

Cartman looks happy! Everybody else looks worried.

CARTMAN
REALLY! YOU CAN?!

MEPHESTO
Yes! Of course... I mean, that much testing will
cost a pretty penny... but.

CARTMAN
How much?

MEPHESTO
Three thousand should cover it!

CARTMAN
I don't have three thousand dollars!

MEPHESTO (cont'd)
Oh, never mind.

Everyone just turns around and starts drinking.

ACT III

EXT. BUS STOP - DAY

STAN
Dude, I can't wait to win that ten thousand dollars on 'America's Stupidest Home Videos'! I'm gonna buy the coolest go-cart ever!

KYLE
I'm gonna buy a walkman with MY half!

Cartman walks up, with his head down.

CARTMAN
(Very slow and sad)
Hey guys.

STAN
How's it going, Cartman?

CARTMAN
Oh... Fine. How are you guys?

The boys can't believe how mellow and normal Cartman is.

KYLE
Dude, what the hell is wrong with you?

CARTMAN
Oh, nothing, it's just - Nothing...

STAN
Come on, what's the matter, Cartman?

CARTMAN
Well, I want to know who my dad is. But to find out, they have to do these DNA tests, and that costs three thousand dollars. I don't have three thousand dollars...

Stan and Kyle look at each other.

STAN
Wow, we're sorry your mom's a whore, dude!

CARTMAN
Yeah, it sucks. I have to know who my father is. I just have to. Maybe I could work at a sweat shop for a while... Well, see you guys, I'm gonna go play in my back yard for a while...

Now Stan and Kyle look really guilty.

KYLE
Uh... Cartman, we know how we can get you three thousand dollars.

CARTMAN
You do?

STAN
Yeah... We have a videotape that's in the finals for 'America's Stupidest Home Videos'... And... And if we win, we'll GIVE you three thousand of our ten-thousand-dollar prize!

CARTMAN
You will?! WOW!! You guys are the BEST!!! THANKS, YOU GUYS!!

STAN
Uh... Yeah.

EXT. CARTMAN'S HOUSE - ESTABLISHING

INT. CARTMAN'S HOUSE

Stan and Kyle and Cartman are gathered in front of the television, enthralled.

NARRATOR
And now back to 'America's Stupidest Home Videos'!!

CARTMAN
What kind of video did you guys make?

STAN
Uh... You'll see.

INT. TELEVISION STUDIO - NIGHT

BOB SAGET
Well, it's time to crown the ten-thousand-dollar winner. Our judges have narrowed it down to only three videos. First, it's: 'Dog who puts hat on master's head'!

Applause.

ANGLE - VIDEO SCREEN

We see a lame video clip of a little dog.

BOB SAGET
(High voice)
Oh, I'm a little dog. I'm just a little dog. Oh, oh!

The dog puts a hat on a bald guy's head.

BOB SAGET (cont'd)
(High voice)
Oh, I've got to put a hat on my master's head, ha, ha!

Back in the studio, the audience is laughing wildly. CLOSE UP on one woman in a 3/4 view laughing so hard, she's crying.

BOB SAGET
And now our second finalist...
'LITTLE BOY HAS A TEA PARTY'!!

Applause.

INT. CARTMAN'S HOUSE

Cartman's eyes widen.

ANGLE - VIDEO SCREEN

The tape of Cartman comes up, he's pouring tea for Polly Prissy Pants.

CARTMAN
(on the monitor)
'Why thank you Polly Prissy Pants, you are my best friend.'

CARTMAN
(in Polly voice)
'Oh thank you Eric.'

The audience howls with laughter.

INT. CARTMAN'S HOUSE

Cartman can't believe it.

BOB SAGET
Boy, it looks like THIS kid needs some therapy!!

Cartman's eyes are HUGE his teeth are clenched.

ANGLE - VIDEO SCREEN

The audience erupts with laughter as little Eric pours tea for his stuffed animals.

STAN
We're sure to win, Cartman! Then you get your DNA money!

CARTMAN
(Shaking violently)
I... AM... SO... PISSED... OFF... RIGHT... NAAAAA!!!!

KYLE
They laughed hardest at our video!
We're gonna win! We're gonna win!!

INT. T.V. STUDIO - DAY

BOB SAGET
And finally, our third contestant,
'Young child gets hit by a train'!!

ANGLE - VIDEO SCREEN

The image comes up. Sure enough, it's Kenny. Somebody videotaped him trying to get the go-cart started.

BOB SAGET
(High voice)
Oh, I'm such a cute little kid.
Hmmm... I wonder if I can get this go-cart started?

ANGLE - CARTMAN'S

The boys watch on in disbelief.

ANGLE - VIDEO SCREEN

We again see the horrific dragging of Kenny. He stops on the train tracks, checks his head, then gets pummeled by the train. In the TV studio, the audience is laughing heartily.

STAN
Oh my God! They've videotaped killing Kenny!!!

KYLE
YOU BASTARDS!!!

The audience is still laughing.

BOB SAGET
Now THAT'S what I call a joy ride!

The audience laughs even harder.

BOB SAGET
And the winner is, naturally...
'Little boy being hit by a train'!!

Applause.

INT. CARTMAN'S HOUSE

STAN
Dude! We LOST!!

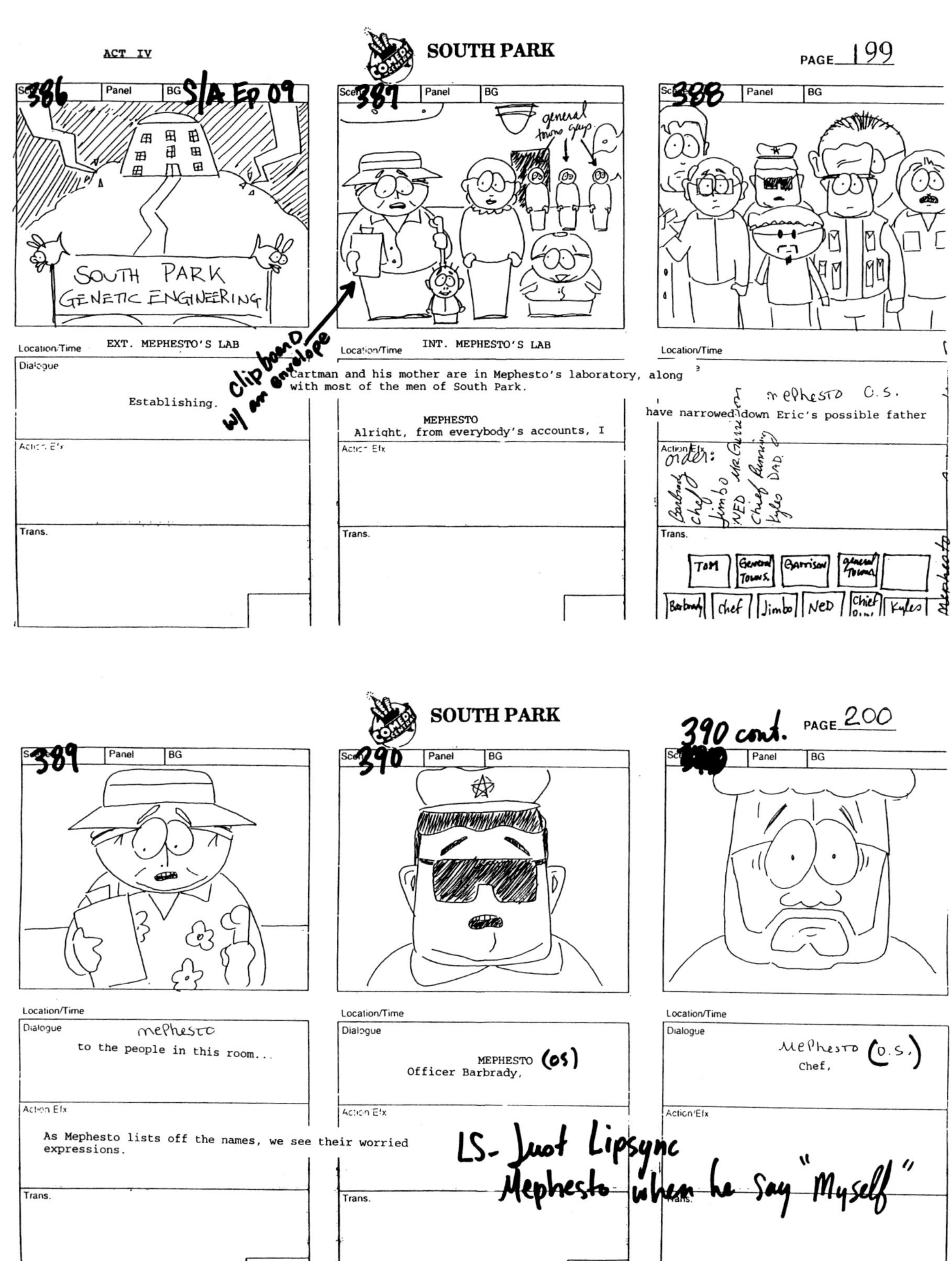
ACT IV
SOUTH PARK
PAGE 199
Scene 386 Panel BG S/A Ep 09
SOUTH PARK GENETIC ENGINEERING
Location/Time EXT. MEPHESTO'S LAB
Dialogue
Establishing.
Action Efx
Trans.
Scene 387 Panel BG
general towns guys
clipboard w/ an envelope
Location/Time INT. MEPHESTO'S LAB
Cartman and his mother are in Mephesto's laboratory, along with most of the men of South Park.
MEPHESTO
Alright, from everybody's accounts, I
Action Efx
Trans.
Scene 388 Panel BG
Location/Time
Mephesto O.S.
have narrowed down Eric's possible father
Action Efx
order:
Barbrady
chef
Jimbo
MR. Garrison
NED
Chief Running
Kyles DAD.
Trans.
TOM
General Towns
Garrison
general towns
Barbrady
chef
Jimbo
NED
Chief
Kyles
Mephesto
SOUTH PARK
390 cont.
PAGE 200
Scene 389 Panel BG
Location/Time
Dialogue
mephesto
to the people in this room...
Action Efx
As Mephesto lists off the names, we see their worried expressions.
Trans.
Scene 390 Panel BG
Location/Time
Dialogue
MEPHESTO (OS)
Officer Barbrady,
Action Efx
Trans.
Scene Panel BG
Location/Time
Dialogue
Mephesto (O.S.)
Chef,
Action Efx
LS- Just Lipsync Mephesto when he say "Myself"
Trans.

KYLE
DAMMIT!!!

CARTMAN
I... AM... GOING... TO... FUCKING... KILL...
YOU GUYS... SERIOUSLY...

INT. T.V. STUDIO - DAY

BOB SAGET
Stand up and take a bow, Mr. Marsh.

Stan's grandfather stands up in the crowd and waves.

GRANDPA
I won! I won!

INT. CARTMAN'S HOUSE

STAN
Grandpa!!!

INT. T.V. STUDIO - DAY

BOB SAGET
Our other finalists will have to settle for
their three-thousand-dollar runner-up prizes.
Well, see you next time!

INT. CARTMAN'S HOUSE

KYLE
Did you hear that, dude?! We still get three thousand
dollars!! That's enough for you to get your DNA tests!!

Cartman is catatonic.

CARTMAN
KILL... YOU GUYS... KILL YOU GUUUYYYYSSSS!!!!!

ACT IV

EXT. MEPHESTO'S LAB

Establishing.

INT. MEPHESTO'S LAB

Cartman and his mother are in Mephesto's laboratory,
along with most of the men of South Park.

MEPHESTO
Alright, from everyone's accounts, I have narrowed down
Eric's possible father to the people in this room...

As Mephesto lists off the names,
we see their worried expressions.

MEPHESTO
Officer Barbrady, Chef, Jimbo, Mr. Garrison, Ned, Chief Running Water, Gerald BROSLOFSKI, Myself, my friend Kevin, or the 1989 Denver Broncos.

The little monkey guy looks worried.
The Broncos all look worried, too.

STAN
Wow, I always knew Cartman's mom was a slut, but God damn!

MEPHESTO
The test results are in this envelope... Shall I open it?

MR. GARRISON
Yes! For God's sake get on with it!!

Mephesto opens the envelope and reads the paper inside.
His expression grows huge.

MEPHESTO
The father of Eric Cartman is INDEED someone in this room!!

Everybody looks around nervously.

MEPHESTO
The father is...

A drum roll starts. The camera starts to focus on different people in the room.

NARRATOR
Who is Eric Cartman's father?
Is it... Chief Running Water?!

Chief looks around nervously.

NARRATOR
Or is it... Chef?!

NARRATOR
Is it Mephesto? Or that little monkey guy that follows him around?

The little monkey guy raises his eyebrows.

NARRATOR
Or is it Mr. Garrison?!

JIMBO
No, he's gay!

MR. GARRISON
You go to hell! You go to hell and you die!!

NARRATOR
Is it Jimbo?

JIMBO
Agh!

NARRATOR
Or is it Officer Barbrady?

OFFICER BARBRADY
Huh, where?

NARRATOR
Or could it be Ned?

NED
Could be.

NARRATOR
Or Mr. BROSLOFSKI?

KYLE
Dad! How could you?

NARRATOR
Or is it the 1991 Denver Broncos? THE ANSWER IS COMING ON AN ALL-NEW SOUTH PARK IN JUST FOUR WEEKS!!!

CARTMAN
What? Son of a bitch!

FIN

EPISODE 201

CARTMAN'S MOM IS STILL A DIRTY SLUT

BY DAVE GOODMAN & TREY PARKER

ACT I

INT. MEPHESTO'S LAB

NARRATOR
Previously, on 'South Park'...

The scene is just as we had left it on episode 113.

NARRATOR
An air of sobriety fills the laboratory as the men of South Park gather to find out which one of them fathered this boy -

ANGLE - CARTMAN

Cartman bites into a doughnut and sips at a drink.

NARRATOR
Who is Eric Cartman's father? At the end of tonight's episode, you WILL KNOW the answer!!

ROLL SOUTH PARK OPENING SEQUENCE

EXT. MEPHESTO'S LAB - NIGHT

Establishing.

INT. MEPHESTO'S LAB

Everyone is gathered around in Mephesto's office, waiting in anticipation.

MEPHESTO
And now... To continue, the father is indeed someone in this room!

CARTMAN
Man, this feels like the longest minute of my life!

Stan and Kyle stand there waiting. Kenny suddenly appears next to them.

STAN
(Confused)
Oh, hey Kenny...

Mephesto takes out the card and reads it.

MEPHESTO
Gentlemen, the father is...

Everyone's eyes get big. Music SWELLS. But then, suddenly, the lights go out!

MR. GARRISON
(In darkness)
Hey, what the hell's going on?

JIMBO
It's a power outage!

Suddenly, we hear BANG! BANG! BANG-BANG!

The lights come back on, and everyone looks around.

CHEF
Is everybody okay? That sounded like a gunshot!

OFFICER BARBRADY
Oh my God! LOOK!!

Mephesto is lying on the floor,
bleeding from gunshot wounds.

KENNY
(Oh my God! They've killed Mephesto!)
Mph mm Mrm! Mrphph mrph MrphMprhMrph!!

KYLE
You bastards!

MR. GARRISON
Mephesto's been shot!!

Everyone rushes over to Mephesto's body.

CHEF
Is he dead?!

JIMBO
Hey, this window is shot out, too! That means the killer
was NOT somebody in this room!

MR. GARRISON
Then who was it?!

Suddenly, the narrator's voice bursts in again.

NARRATOR
(V.O.)
Who shot Mephesto? Was it the school counselor?
(As pictures fly past)
Or was it Ms. Crabtree? Or was it -

CARTMAN
Hey! Wait a minute! I didn't find out who my father was!

NARRATOR (cont'd)
(Pictures continue)
Or was it Ms. Broslofski?

Chef is leaning down by Mephesto.

CHEF
Wait! He's still breathing! He's not dead!

A few people help Chef lift up Mephesto and lead him towards the door. Cartman gets in Mephesto's face.

CARTMAN
GOD DAMMIT! WHO'S MY FATHER?!

But Mephesto is not conscious.

CHEF
We have to get him to the hospital!

CARTMAN
You've got to be kidding me!!!!

CHEF
Come on, children!

The boys follow Chef out the door.

CARTMAN
Oh!

MR. BROSLOFSKI
Oh, that poor kid. It must be hell for him going through all this.

Ms. Cartman is standing right next to him. When she hears this, she lowers her head and walks away.

JIMBO
There's a murderer free in South Park!
We have to find out who it is before they kill again!

MR. GARRISON
Yeah, God only knows who they'll kill next!

NARRATOR
Who will they kill next? Will it be Jimbo?
(Slides again)
Barbrady? The Denver Broncos...?

INT. CHEF'S CAR - NIGHT

Chef drives with Cartman in the front seat and the boys in back, with an unconscious Mephesto in the way back.

CARTMAN
Is he awake yet?

KYLE
He's bleeding pretty bad back here.

CHEF
Don't let him bleed on my Meredith Baxter Birney memorial towel.

KYLE
What's a Meredith Baxter Birney memorial towel?

CHEF
I actually was with Meredith Baxter Birney in this very car, and afterwards, we used that towel to... Wait a minute, why am I telling you this?

Meanwhile, Stan is looking incredibly sick.

STAN
Could you pull over so I can get out?

CHEF
What? We have to get to the hospital!

STAN
I have to get out first, I'm not gonna make it. I can't stand hospitals!

CHEF
Sorry, Stan. We just gotta drop Mephesto off, and then we can get out of there, alright?

KYLE
Man, it's really starting to snow, I hope they don't close the roads.

CARTMAN
They can't! Mephesto can't die!!!

KYLE
Maybe it's better you don't know who your father is, Cartman.

CARTMAN
No way, dude, I can't stand to leave things unfinished. It's like when you hear the first part of that song 'Come Sail Away' by Styx. If I hear the first part of that song I have to finish it.

Everybody looks at each other, confused.

KYLE
Really?

CARTMAN
Yeah. I can't do anything until it's done.

KYLE
'I'm sailingg awayyy...'

CARTMAN
No! Don't!

KYLE
'Set an open course for the Virgin Sea...'

Kyle stops abruptly. Cartman sits and shakes. He turns red like he's trying desperately to hold back. Finally, his mouth opens and it comes bursting forth.

CARTMAN
- 'Cause I've got to be free to carry on.
Duh-dun, (and so on)

KYLE
Woa, dude!

EXT. MOUNTAIN ROAD - DAY

Chef's car speeds up the mountain road.

A small, single snowflake falls from the sky and lands on the sign that reads 'Hell's Pass Hospital - 35 miles'.

OMINOUS MUSIC STING.

INT. MAYOR'S OFFICE - NIGHT

Everyone is gathered in the Mayor's Office.
She tries to calm them down.

JIMBO
What are we going to do, Mayor?
This killer is on the loose!!

KYLE'S MOTHER
We can't even leave our homes for fear
of our children's safety!

STAN'S MOTHER
Uh... Where are our children?

Everyone looks around.

MAYOR
Officer Barbrady... Let's pretend for one second
that we had a competent law enforcer in this town.
What would HE do?

BARBRADY
Hmm... That's a good question, Mayor...
Let me get right on that with thinking.

Barbrady goes into a trance. Suddenly, a crew of people carrying film equipment rush in.

DIRECTOR
Mayor! Mayor!

MAYOR
The press is here!

DIRECTOR
My name is Sid Greenfield. I'm the director from Los Angeles for 'America's Most Wanted'.

MAYOR
You certainly made it up here quickly.

DIRECTOR
We're desperate for stories.
(Catching himself)
AND this one is so compelling!

MAYOR
Really?

DIRECTOR
Sure! This story has everything! People... furniture... talking... It's a real American story.

BARBRADY
Hey, I thought of something!
(Pause)
Er... No wait, that's subtraction...

MAYOR
(Ignoring this)
Mr. Director person, what exactly do you want to do?

JIMBO
Mayor, shouldn't we be focusing on -

MAYOR
Shh!

DIRECTOR
We just want to do a recreation of the story for our show. Then we'll flash a number on the screen that people can call if they have any information regarding the identity or location of the shooter. That's it. You win. We win. America wins.

MAYOR
Are you sure this wouldn't make our little town look dangerous?

DIRECTOR
Don't worry, Mayor, 'America's Most Wanted' is not about violence, it's about family.

CAMERA GUY
It is?

MAYOR
Well, in that case, I guess it's okay.

DIRECTOR
Great! We'll get started with auditions immediately. What part should we cast first?

Again the Narrator's voice bursts in.

NARRATOR
WHO WILL THE DIRECTOR CAST FIRST?! WILL IT BE MR. GARRISON? OFFICER BARBRADY? CHEF...?

EXT. UNPLANNED PARENTHOOD - DAY

The snow falls on this small, humble clinic.

MS. CARTMAN
(V.O.)
I want to have an abortion.

INT. UNPLANNED PARENTHOOD - DAY

SOCIAL WORKER
Oh, well we can do that. This must be a very difficult time for you Ms...

MS. CARTMAN
Cartman... Yes, It's such a hard decision. But I just don't feel I can raise a child in this screwy world.

SOCIAL WORKER
Yes, Ms. Cartman, if you don't feel fit to raise a child, an abortion probably is the answer. Do you know the actual time of conception?

MS. CARTMAN
About eight years ago.

The Social Worker looks confused.

SOCIAL WORKER
I see... So the fetus is...

MS. CARTMAN
Eight years old.

SOCIAL WORKER
Ms. Cartman, eight years old is a little late to be considering abortion.

MS. CARTMAN
Really?

SOCIAL WORKER
Yes, this is what we would refer to as the FORTIETH trimester.

MS. CARTMAN
But I just don't think I'm a fit mother.

SOCIAL WORKER
Well, but we prefer to abort babies a little earlier on. In fact, there's a law against abortions after the second trimester.

MS. CARTMAN
Well... I think you need to keep your laws off of my body.

SOCIAL WORKER
Hmmm... I'm afraid I can't help you, Ms. Cartman. If you want to change the law, you'll have to speak with your congressman.

MS. CARTMAN
(A little pissed)
Well, then that's EXACTLY what I intend to do! Good day!

EXT. HELL'S PASS HOSPITAL - DAY

Chef's car pulls up. Snow is falling heavily.

CHEF
Come on children, we gotta find a doctor!

Stan stops at the door.

STAN
I can't do it, dude!

KYLE
Come on, Stan. Hospitals aren't all that bad.

CARTMAN
Yeah, stop being a wuss.

INT. HELL'S PASS HOSPITAL - NIGHT

Chef and the children enter to find a doctor and nurse standing over a patient in the ER.

CHEF
Doctor!

DOCTOR
One moment please! NURSE! I need twenty CCs of sodium pentothal, STAT!!

The nurse runs over to the surgical tray. She has no arms, however, and must pick up the syringe with her teeth.

KYLE
Woa, dude, she doesn't have any arms!

DOCTOR
We're an equal opportunity employer here, son.

The nurse spits the syringe into the doctor's hands.

CHEF
Doctor, we've got a shot cracker outside!

DOCTOR
I'll be with you right after I inject this man with a long needle.

STAN
Oh man, I'm gonna be sick...

DOCTOR
There, there, young man. Medical science is nothing to be afraid of.

To remove the air from the syringe, the doctor squirts out a long stream of pentothal.

STAN
UGH!

The doctor injects the patient.

NURSE GOODLY
Oooh, I think you're hitting the bone!!

STAN
(Turning blue)
AAGHH!

DOCTOR
Yeah, I can hear the needle scraping against the bone inside!

Sccccrrrreeeee.....

DOCTOR (cont'd)
Oops, he's hemorrhaging!

A long, thick arc of blood squirts through the air and hits the ground next to Stan. Now, for absolutely no reason, the patient's head falls off and hits the ground.

DOCTOR
Oops! His head fell off!

STAN
I'm gettin' outta here!!!

KYLE
Stan!

DOCTOR
Well, some people just have a weak stomach.

EXT. 'AMERICA'S MOST WANTED' HEADQUARTERS - NIGHT

Establishing.

AMW has not set up a little trailer, but a huge complex with a sign: AMERICA'S MOST WANTED: SOUTH PARK HEADQUARTERS.

INT. AUDITORIUM

The Director sits in the dimly lit theatre seats, listening to actors as they audition for parts. A sign on the small stage reads 'America's Most Wanted Auditions'. A very average-looking man, wearing Mephesto's Hawaiian shirt is on the stage, reading from a script.

MEPHESTO ACTOR
And the father of Eric Cartman is... BANG! Ugh!! Jimminy! I've been shot!!

DIRECTOR
Oh, thank you very much, we'll get back to you.

The actor leaves.

DIRECTOR
I think I've seen enough genetic engineers.
Let's move on to the auditions for the part of...
(Looking at papers)
Mr.... Garrison.

ASSISTANT DIRECTOR
Call the Mr. Garrison auditions!!

A young actor comes out with a sock on his hand.

ACTOR
Boy, I sure hope I'm not Eric Cartman's father, Mr. Hat.
(As Mr. Hat)
You can say that again, Mr. Garrison.

DIRECTOR
Alright, not bad. Let's keep him on the top pile. Next!

Mr. Garrison walks out.

MR. GARRISON
I sure hope that I am not Eric Cartman's father, Mr. Hat.
(As Mr. Hat)
You can say that again, Mr. Garrison.

DIRECTOR
Thank you - NEXT!

MR. GARRISON
What?

DIRECTOR
NEXT!

Garrison looks puzzled and walks away.
A very good-looking actor takes his place.

GOOD-LOOKING ACTOR
I sure hope that I am not Eric Cartman's father, Mr. Hat.
(As Mr. Hat)
You can say that again, Mr. Garrison.

DIRECTOR
PERFECT! YOU GOT IT!!

Mr. Garrison exchanges looks with Mr. Hat.

DIRECTOR (cont'd)
Let's move on to the Chefs!

INT. BEDROOM - NIGHT

Ms. Cartman is lying naked in bed with a clean-cut gentleman, who is smoking a cigarette.

MS. CARTMAN
And so you see Congressman O'Riley, that's why I think abortion laws should be changed.

CONGRESSMAN
Well, all I know is that third trimester abortions are illegal. I don't really know anything about fortieth.

MS. CARTMAN
But the person at Unplanned Parenthood said you were who I had to talk to about changing the law.

CONGRESSMAN
No, no, I think you gotta talk to the Governor about that stuff.

MS. CARTMAN
Oh dear.

EXT. HOSPITAL - NIGHT

We see Chef's car being buried by the heavy snowfall.

INT. EMERGENCY ROOM - NIGHT

Chef and Cartman and the boys stand around a bed where Mephesto is lying, hooked up to all kinds of machines.

DOCTOR
Well, this is about all I can do for him.

CARTMAN
Can't you get him to talk? I have to know who my father is!!

DOCTOR
Sorry, son, it might be a while.

Cartman jumps up on Mephesto and starts slapping him in the face.

CARTMAN
WAKE UP YOU SON OF A BITCH!!!!

CHEF
WOA!

DOCTOR
(Pulling him off)
Now, son, that's not gonna do him any good. I'll let you know if there's a change in his condition.

CARTMAN
I CAN'T WAIT ANYMORE!! WHAT AM I SUPPOSED TO DO?!?!

KYLE
Hey, Cartman...

CARTMAN
What?

KYLE
'I'mmmmm sailinngg aw-'

Kyle stops. Cartman's eyes grow wide. He starts to shake.

CARTMAN
'-way set an open course on the Virgin Sea.' (continues)

STAN
Okay, okay. Let's get out of here now.

KYLE
I don't know if that's gonna be too easy...

Kyle is looking out the window, where the blizzard has intensified. Chef's car is completely buried.

DOCTOR
My God, that's a hell of a storm.

STAN
Oh, weak...

EXT. 'AMERICA'S MOST WANTED' HEADQUARTERS

Snow has started to fall in South Park.

INT. 'AMERICA'S MOST WANTED' HEADQUARTERS

The Director is looking out the window at the falling snow.

DIRECTOR
God I hate mountains. This better not push back our shooting schedule.

Now the Director steps back, and we see that he is next to a huge facade of Mephesto's lab. Movie cameras and lights abound. A full cast is on hand, with actors dressed up as all the main characters.

DIRECTOR
Okay people, let's rehearse the reenactment from the top before we shoot it.

Everyone takes their places.

DIRECTOR (cont'd)
Who's that?

Eric Roberts is wearing a Hawaiian shirt and walking around.

ASSISTANT
Oh that's T.V.'s Eric Roberts, we were able to get him to play the part of the little monkey guy.

DIRECTOR
Oooh, talk about washed up, huh?
(To Eric, louder)
Great to have you, Eric!

Eric waves.

DIRECTOR
Here we go... And... ACTION!!

MEPHESTO ACTOR
I want to announce who the father is -

DIRECTOR
BANG!

MEPHESTO ACTOR
Oh! I've been shot!

BARBRADY ACTOR
Nobody move! I'm a law officer!

CHEF ACTOR
My God... I think he's gone into cardiac arrest.

BARBRADY ACTOR
You seem somewhat unnerved by this, Chef.

CHEF ACTOR
Are you accusing me, Barbrady? Because if you are, accuse! Don't hide behind your clever riddles.

BARBRADY ACTOR
Our differences must be set aside for now, Mr. Chef. I'm simply a man. A man trying to do my job.

The South Park townspeople are watching from behind the cameras.

OFFICER BARBRADY
Woa, this is a good movie!

INT. EMERGENCY ROOM - NIGHT

Chef and the boys are sitting in the waiting room, bored, with a plethora of injured people waiting to get attention. Stan looks to his left where a man is holding his stabbed arm with the knife still in it. He grimaces and looks to his right where a woman is bleeding out her jugular.

CARTMAN
'Sail away with meeee!!!!'

Cartman takes a deep breath, satisfied.

STAN
Ohhh, dude, when can we get out of here?

The doctor rushes in and starts tending to the next patient.

JUGULAR WOMAN
Doctor! I can't focus!

DOCTOR
We're doing the best we can, ma'am. They've closed the pass and none of the other doctors can get through. For now it's just me and Nurse Goodly.

Nurse Goodly fumbles around for a stethoscope sans arms.

CHEF
Wait a second, they've closed the pass?

DOCTOR
Yes. I'm afraid we're critically understaffed. Unless we get help soon, all these people in here are completely fucked.

The patients all look at the doctor with worry. A hush falls over them.

DOCTOR
(To them)
Metaphorically speaking, that is.

CARTMAN
What about Mephesto?! Are you taking care of him?!

DOCTOR
He's on full life-support and breathing fine. He shouldn't need any help... So long as the power doesn't go out.

The power goes out.

Everyone just stands there in complete darkness.

DOCTOR
Whoof, who didn't see that coming a mile away, huh?

ACT II

ROLL 'AMERICA'S MOST WANTED' INTRODUCTION SEQUENCE

MUSIC. A sequence of chase and arrest scenes, flashing lights and running cops and robbers.

NARRATOR
Tonight, on 'America's Most Wanted', a shooter is on the loose in Colorado, and the residents are up in arms! Here's your host, John Walsh.

JOHN WALSH
Good evening and welcome to 'America's Most Wanted'. Tonight, terror invaded the small mountain community of South Park Colorado when Dr. Alphonse Mephesto was gunned down in his laboratory. 'America's Most Wanted' has reconstructed this heinous crime in hopes that your calls can help solve the case.

INT. MEPHESTO'S LAB SET - NIGHT

Thunder and lightning blast outside as we see all the actors in their respective costumes.

MEPHESTO ACTOR
I've been shot!!

MR. GARRISON ACTOR
My God, Mr. Hat, get some help.

MR. HAT ACTOR
(A tall, handsome actor)
Right away, Mr. Garrison.

ERIC ROBERTS
No! Noo!! My lifetime partner and friend. Gone, taken away in the wink of an eye! Oh, fortune! How you mock me!

DIRECTOR
What the?! Eric Roberts is improving lines again!

CHEF ACTOR
I'm going to get the man to a hospital. Who will help me?

ERIC ROBERTS
This is not a world I want to live in! It is an angry world.

DIRECTOR
Dammit!!

Just then, all the power goes out.

EXT. 'AMERICA'S MOST WANTED' HEADQUARTERS

A tree has blown over on the power lines. They spark in the falling snow.

INT. 'AMERICA'S MOST WANTED' HEADQUARTERS

DIRECTOR
What the hell is this?!

CAMERA GUY
We've lost the feed to L.A.!

INT. 'AMERICA'S MOST WANTED' HEADQUARTERS IN L.A.

John Walsh is still standing there, but with all the screens static.

JOHN WALSH
Uhh... We seem to have lost our linkup to the South Park crew... So I guess we'll be going to our feature movie, 'Who Framed Roger Rabbit'.

ANNOUNCER
Who framed Roger Rabbit? Was it Jimbo? Mr. Garrison? Chef?

INT. 'AMERICA'S MOST WANTED' HEADQUARTERS

DIRECTOR
Somebody go see why we lost the hookup!

Just then, the door blows open and snow flies everywhere.

JIMBO
Holy smokes! That blizzard is gettin' crazy!

EXT. HOSPITAL OF DOOM - NIGHT

The snow has absolutely buried the hospital. The eerie moonlight makes the place look like something out of 'The Shining'.

INT. EMERGENCY ROOM - NIGHT

The emergency lights have come on, but are noticably dimmer. All the patients are screaming and running around in horror.

NURSE GOODLY
Don't panic, anybody. The power lines are down, but the backup generator is running fine.

The doctor pops out from the E.R.

DOCTOR
Nurse! I could use some help in here!

NURSE GOODLY
Coming!

But as the nurse heads towards the doctor, Cartman steps in front of her.

CARTMAN
Lady, is Mephesto going to be okay?

NURSE GOODLY
Yes... For now. But I'm afraid the generator won't run for long. The batteries run out in half an hour. Time is very short.

DOCTOR
Nurse, PLEASE! I need another pair of HANDS in here!!
(Beat)
Oh... Sorry.

INT. ANOTHER BEDROOM - NIGHT

In a very immaculate bedroom, Ms. Cartman is again lying naked next to a naked older-looking man. He's smoking a cigarette.

MS. CARTMAN
Don't you see, Govenor? I should have a right to have an abortion if I want one.

GOVENOR
Mmm... I don't know, I might need some more convincing.

He rolls over and puts his arm around her.

MS. CARTMAN
I mean, what right do I have bringing another child into this overpopulated world? Then again, I should have thought of that before having sex... Then again... Oh, I just don't know!

INT. HOSPITAL - NIGHT

Stan and Kyle are back with Chef, who is talking to the doctor.

DOCTOR
Please, Mr. Chef, I have over a hundred people to tend to here, and only myself and Nurse Goodly.

CHEF
What do you want me to do?

DOCTOR
Do you know anything about surgery?

CHEF
I used to watch 'Quincy'.

DOCTOR
WHAT?! Why the hell didn't you say so! Put on some scrubs!!

The doctor turns to the boys.

DOCTOR
Boys, I'm making you all honorary doctors!
You can help us save these people's lives!

Stan gets a very, very worried look on his face.

STAN
No way, dude!

EXT. 'AMERICA'S MOST WANTED' HEADQUARTERS - NIGHT

The snow is piled high all around 'America's Most Wanted'.
Everything is absolutely covered.

INT. 'AMERICA'S MOST WANTED' HEADQUARTERS

Jimbo opens the front door. A huge mound of snow rushes
in, and blowing snow flies in his face.

JIMBO
Well, we're not going anywhere for a long time.

DIRECTOR
We're snowed in?

MAYOR
Yes... We're TRAPPED.

MR. GARRISON
Like sailors on a submarine.

Garrison looks at the Director.

MAYOR
My God, this is the worst storm I've ever seen.

ASSISTANT DIRECTOR
Ohh, I have to get out of here,
I haven't eaten since breakfast.

OFFICER BARBRADY
Yeah, I'm gettin' hungry too.

JIMBO
I hope you all realize what we might be facing here...

Everyone looks at Jimbo.

JIMBO
Our only option might be to EAT EACH OTHER to stay alive!

MUSIC STING. Everybody GASPS.

SOUTH PARK
PAGE 115
Scene 274 Panel BG S/A 269
Location/Time
Dialogue
Jimbo (Cont'd)
(alive) so be it.
Action/Efx
Trans.
27
Scene 275 Panel BG S/A 264
Dialogue
MAYOR
But how do we decide... who?
Action/Efx
Trans.
64
Scene 276 Panel BG S/A 269
Dialogue
JIMBO
We draw straws.
Action/Efx
Trans.
34
SOUTH PARK
PAGE 116
Scene 277 Panel BG
Dialogue
DIRECTOR
(Hysterical)
Now wait a minute! We all had a big breakfast,
Action/Efx
Trans.
50
Scene 278 Panel BG S/A 271
Dialogue
Director
can't you people go without eating for a little-
Action/Efx
Trans.
58
Scene 279 Panel BG S/A 269
Dialogue
JIMBO
CALM DOWN, SOLDIER!! WE NEED EVERY PERSON HERE TO KEEP HIS HEAD!!
Action/Efx
Trans.
79

DIRECTOR
Uhh... It's only been like four hours. Aren't you resorting to cannibalism a little quickly?

JIMBO
That's the law of the land, Mr. Director. I know it ain't pretty, but if a few of us might die so that the rest can stay alive, so be it.

MAYOR
But how do we decide... who?

JIMBO
Well, we draw straws.

DIRECTOR
(Hysterical)
Now wait a minute! We all had a big breakfast, can't you people go without eating for a little while?

JIMBO
CALM DOWN, SOLDIER!! WE NEED EVERY PERSON HERE TO KEEP HIS HEAD!! Barbrady, fetch some straws.

DIRECTOR
Well who the hell made you the boss anyway?!

Jimbo opens his mouth to answer, when -

ANNOUNCER
Who the hell made Jimbo boss? Was it Barbrady? Chef? Mr. Garrison?

INT. EMERGENCY ROOM - NIGHT

The doctor is standing over a patient, who is lying on an operating table.

DOCTOR
This man's appendix has burst. I have no choice but to operate now, with our limited power. I need you all to be strong for me.

Chef and the boys are wearing scrubs and holding their hands in the air. Stan is absolutely green with nausea.

DOCTOR
Okay. Nurse Goodly will take care of anaesthesia. Chef, you'll act as her arms. Boys, you have to help with suction and bandages. Ready?

STAN
No.

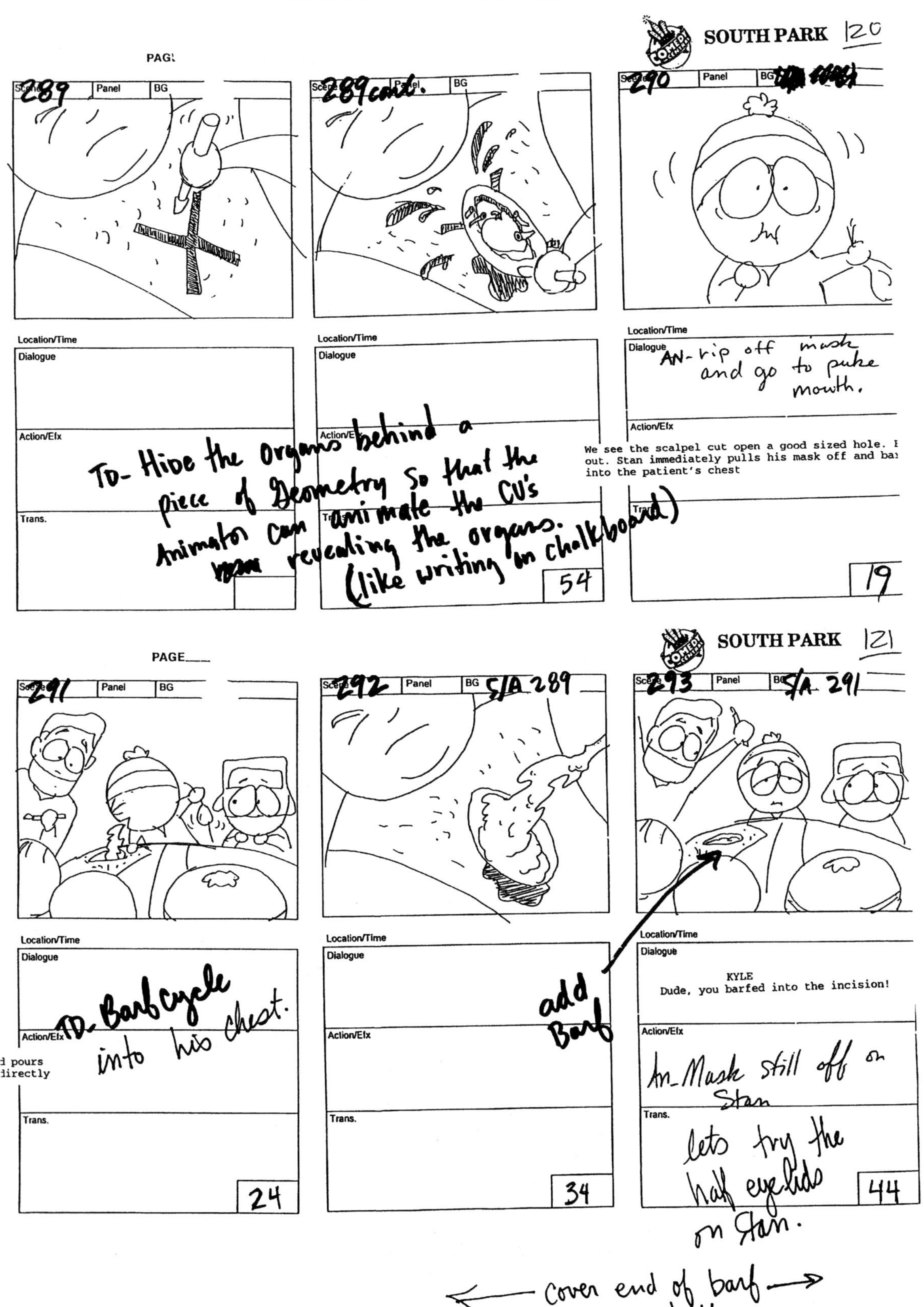
SOUTH PARK 120
PAGE
Scene 289 Panel BG
Scene 289 cont. Panel BG
Scene 290 Panel BG
Location/Time
Dialogue
Action/Efx
Trans.
Dialogue AN- rip off mask and go to puke mouth.
Action/Efx
We see the scalpel cut open a good sized hole. I out. Stan immediately pulls his mask off and ba into the patient's chest
TO- Hide the organs behind a piece of Geometry so that the Animator can animate the CU's revealing the organs. (like writing on chalkboard)
54
19
SOUTH PARK 121
PAGE___
Scene 291 Panel BG
Scene 292 Panel BG S/A 289
Scene 293 Panel BG S/A 291
Location/Time
Dialogue
TD- Barf cycle into his chest.
Action/Efx
d pours directly
Trans.
24
add Barf
34
KYLE
Dude, you barfed into the incision!
An_Mask still off on Stan
lets try the half eyelids on Stan.
44
cover end of barf in both

DOCTOR
Okay, first I'll make an incision on the chest over the heart.

STAN
Oh, boy.

We see the scalpel cut open a good sized hole. Blood pours out. Stan immediately pulls his mask off and barfs directly into the patient's chest.

KYLE
Dude, you barfed into the incision!

CARTMAN
Sweet!

DOCTOR
(Jumping up and down)
Suction!

Kenny pulls the suction cup over the incision. SSSSLLLUURRPP. Suddenly, the lights begin to dim.

CARTMAN
Hey, who's screwing with the lights?!

The narrator pops up.

NARRATOR
Who IS screwing with the lights?
(Pictured:)
Is it Barbrady? Or Jimbo? Or the 1991 Denver Broncos?

CARTMAN
That is really starting to piss me off.

INT. 'AMERICA'S MOST WANTED' HEADQUARTERS

Everyone is gathered around and drawing straws from Officer Barbrady.

JIMBO
Alright, so far everybody has a long piece of straw. We'll keep drawing...

Jimbo pulls his straw out... It's pretty long. He sighs relief. Mr. Garrison pulls his straw out... It's pretty long. He sighs relief. The Mayor pulls a straw... It's pretty long. She sighs relief.

Barbrady is left with the last piece... He opens his hand... And there's ANOTHER long piece of straw.

SOUTH PARK PAGE______ 135

Scene 331 | Panel | BG

Location/Time

Dialogue

DOCTOR
Team A will consist of myself, Stan, Kyle, Eric, Chef, and Nurse Goodly.

Action/Efx

veryone gathers around and listens closely.

Trans.

115

Scene 332 | Panel | BG

Location/Time

Dialogue

Action/Efx

Trans.

13

Scene 333 | Panel | BG S/A 330

Location/Time 3 Shot. (No Boy

Dialogue Doctor (cont)

Team B will consist of Kenny.

Action/Efx

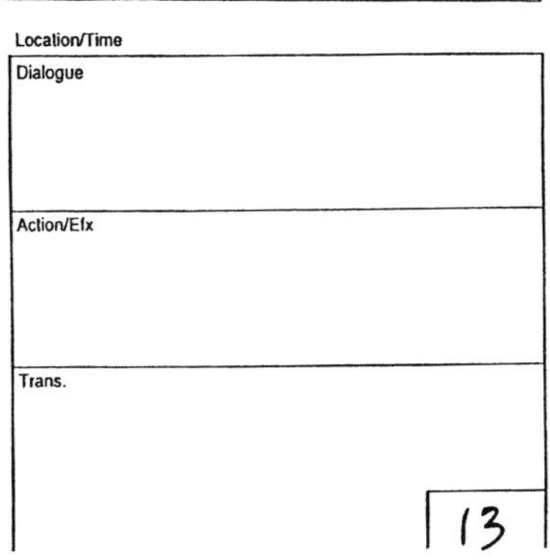

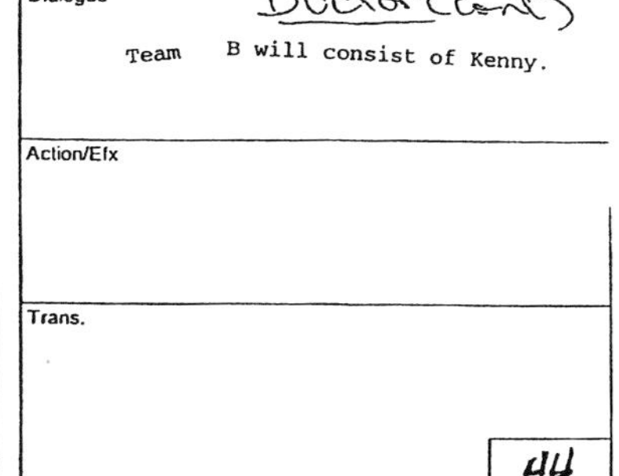

Trans.

44

SOUTH PARK

Scene 334 | Panel | BG

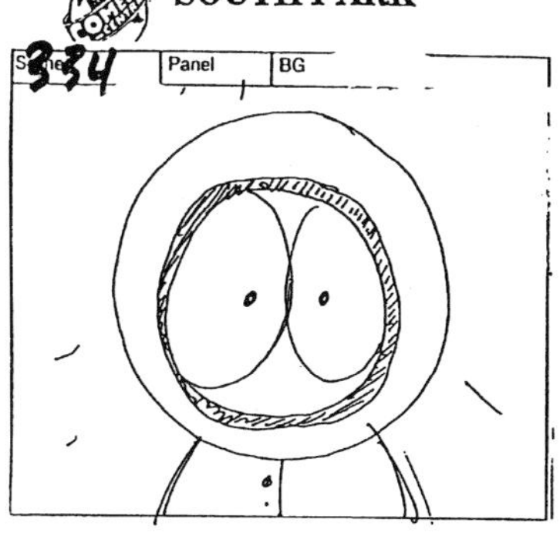

Location/Time

Dialogue

Action/Efx

Kenny's eyes grow wide.

Trans.

26

Scene 335 | Panel | BG S/A 331

Location/Time

Dialogue

DOCTOR
(To Kenny)
Now listen closely, team B.

Action/Efx

AN_ Slow Zoom in

Trans.

38

SOUTH PARK 136

Scene 336 | Panel | BG

Location/Time

Dialogue Doctor

Your goal will be turn on the backup generator.
(MORE)

DOCTOR (cont'd)
To do this, you must brave the storm outside

He p

Trans. AN-Watch Dr.'s arm Continuity for the next Seqvence

106

JIMBO
Whew!

MR. GARRISON
Whew!

OFFICER BARBRADY
Whew!

JIMBO
Wait a minute... Where the hell is the short one?

OFFICER BARBRADY
The short what?

JIMBO
Dammit, Barbrady! When you draw straws you're supposed to have one of 'em short, that's how you decide who loses!

Barbrady thinks.

OFFICER BARBRADY
That's not how I played it.

MR. GARRISON
Ugh... Could we hurry this up, my stomach's growling!

INT. HELL'S PASS HOSPITAL - NIGHT

The doctor enters with large blueprints of the hospital. Dim back-up lights are flickering.

DOCTOR
I found a map that shows the location of a backup generator!

He rolls out the blueprints.

DOCTOR
Apparently they built a large, self-sustaining generator for just this kind of emergency. But it's out and away from the hospital!

CHEF
So how do we get to it?

DOCTOR
We must split up into two teams. Team A and Team B.

Everyone gathers around and listens closely.

DOCTOR
Team A will consist of myself, Stan, Kyle, Eric, Chef, and Nurse Goodly. Team B will consist of Kenny.

Kenny's eyes grow wide.

DOCTOR
(To Kenny)
Now listen closely, Team B. Your goal will be turn on the backup generator. To do this, you must brave the storm outside and get into this sewage duct.

He points to these various areas on the blueprint.

DOCTOR (cont'd)
Meanwhile, Team A will go to the holding area... HERE. Where there is a television and some cocoa. We will drink the cocoa and watch family programming until Team B makes it through the sewage duct.

Kenny looks suspicious.

DOCTOR
By that time, Team B (remember, that's you Kenny) should reach the outer core of the generator. It will be a cold and dangerous climb to the top, and there could be velociraptors HERE.

Kenny panics.

DOCTOR
Once you reach the top, you should be able to get a clear view through THIS window, of us drinking cocoa and watching television. Then you can proceed down into the generator and power it on. Are there any questions?

CARTMAN
No, that sounds pretty sweet to me.

DOCTOR
Right then, let's DO IT!! GO TEAM!!!

KENNY
Hmph?

EXT. 'AMERICA'S MOST WANTED' HEADQUARTERS

Everyone is lying on the dimly lit floor, looking as if they haven't eaten for weeks.

MR. GARRISON
C... Can't go on... S-So h-hungry...

MAYOR
We're all going to die in this horrible place.

JIMBO
We have to have the energy to make it through the night... We have to eat.

DIRECTOR
How can we? How could we live with ourselves?

JIMBO
There's only one answer... Eat Eric Roberts.

Eric Roberts panics.

MAYOR
Yes... Of course. Nobody gives a shit about Eric Roberts.

MR. GARRISON
Eat Eric Roberts...

ERIC ROBERTS
No!

Everybody closes in on Eric Roberts.

ERIC ROBERTS
(cont'd)
No, PLEASE!!

ACT III

INT. 'AMERICA'S MOST WANTED' HEADQUARTERS

Eric Roberts, now nothing but a carcass, lies off to the side. Everyone is quietly huddled around the fire.

MAYOR
Well, there's no going back now...
We're cannibals. God save us.

JIMBO
God wants you to live, Mayor. Fight!

ASSISTANT DIRECTOR
Well, I have to admit, Eric Roberts was much juicer than I expected.

DIRECTOR
Aw!

MR. GARRISON
This snow just isn't letting up.
We're going to die here, I know it.

JIMBO
What time is it, Barbrady?

BARBRADY
(Checking his watch)
It's almost midnight.

MR. GARRISON
Oh, I can't go on...

JIMBO
We'll give the storm another hour. After that...
We might have to eat again...

DRAMATIC MUSIC.

DIRECTOR
What?! Christ, are you people diabetic or something?!

EXT. HOSPITAL - NIGHT

Kenny crawls out of a small duct, covered with sewage. The horrible storm blows around him in all directions, Kenny can barely see. The doctor's voice blasts over Kenny's walkie talkie.

DOCTOR
Team B... Come in, Team B.

KENNY
Mph mh mphm B.

DOCTOR
Listen, Team B, we've found another path to the generator. There's actually a nice, heated walkway to it, so you don't need to walk through all that sewage.

Kenny looks down at his sewage-covered body.

KENNY
(Pissed)
Mph rmph rm rmphm!!!

DOCTOR
Oh... Well forget I said that then. Listen, Team B, you should be seeing a large drift of snow with some metal sticking out of it just to your left...

KENNY
Mph, mpmh mphmh mm.

Kenny spots the snow-covered backup generator.

DOCTOR
Good. Head towards it, Team A out.

CARTMAN
What if Mephesto never wakes up and
I never find out who my father is?

Little Kenny bravely treads through the deep snow, just as the shadow of a velociraptor runs by with a cry.

EXT. 'AMERICA'S MOST WANTED' HEADQUARTERS

Everyone appears to be eating somberly. We see Eric Roberts's nearly skeletal corpse, and next to it, the corpses of the Director and his Assistant.

The Mayor forks over some meat off of the Assistant Director.

MAYOR
My God what a harrowing tale of human drama this is! All of us doing what we must to survive.

JIMBO
It is amazing what people can do under stress. Just look at the pyramids, nobody knows how they built those. Or who.

NARRATOR
Who built the pyramids? Was it the Babylonians? Officer Barbrady? Samaritans?

INT. HOSPITAL - NIGHT

Everyone is gathered around Mephesto's bed. The power appears to still be draining, as the lights dim, and electrical sounds wurr down...

EXT. BACK-UP GENERATOR

KENNY
(On his walkie)
Mmmph mmm mph.

INT. HOSPITAL

DOCTOR
Roger, Team B. He's reached the backup generator. Team B, can you see the two copper nodes?

EXT. BACK-UP GENERATOR

KENNY
(On his walkie)
Mmmph mmm mph.

INT. HOSPITAL

DOCTOR
Good, now is there a wire connecting them?

EXT. BACK-UP GENERATOR

KENNY
Mmm npm.

INT. HOSPITAL

DOCTOR
Damn. The wire connecting the nodes is gone. We need to complete the circuit between them or we're screwed.

KYLE
Do you have any wire here?

DOCTOR
There's no time. Once these lights flicker out. All the patients on life-support are going to die.

EXT. BACK-UP GENERATOR

KENNY
Mrmp mmme mrph.

INT. HOSPITAL

DOCTOR
No Kenny you can't. There must be some other way. He's going to make the connection himself with his hands.

KYLE
No, he'll die!

CARTMAN
Go Kenny.

DOCTOR
Kenny... Nooooooo...

EXT. BACK-UP GENERATOR

Kenny connects the lines with his hands and we see him light up like a Christmas tree.

INT. HOSPITAL

STAN
Oh my God they've killed Kenny!

KYLE
You bastards!

Suddenly the power comes on!!!

CHEF
The power!!

DOCTOR
Quickly, get the scanner running again!!

Everybody converges on Mephesto.

DOCTOR
We've got a chance, now!!

EXT. THE WHITE HOUSE ESTABLISHING

INT. PRESIDENT'S BEDROOM

PRESIDENT
Well okay Mrs. Cartman, I'll legalize fortieth trimester abortions for you.

MS. CARTMAN
Oh thank you, thank you.

PRESIDENT
We'll have the pregnancy terminated immediately.

MS. CARTMAN
Terminated?

PRESIDENT
Oh yes, that's what an abortion is.

MS. CARTMAN
Oh no, I didn't mean that. I meant the other thing you can do. What's that other "A" word?

PRESIDENT
Adoption?

MS. CARTMAN
Yes, that's what I mean. Adoption.

PRESIDENT
Well that's pretty different.

MS. CARTMAN
Oh I should just tell my son the truth about everything myself. Good day Mr. President.

EXT. SOUTH PARK

The sun begins to rise. All over South Park, we see snow slowly melting as the sun's rays drift over the land. A few birds come out and start singing as the light shows us the town of South Park, half-buried in snow.

INT. HOSPITAL - NIGHT

Mephesto's room, now lit by sunlight seems much more pleasant.

DOCTOR
Well, we made it. The power is on, the snow is melting and your friend Mephesto is doing fine.

SOUTH PARK
PAGE 174
430
Generator Reverse
431
431 cont.
tighter
tighter
Location/Time EXT. HOSPITAL - DAY
STAN
He was a good friend, and I'll miss him.
KYLE
He was very brave... He risked his life so that Mephesto could live.
CARTMAN
Yeah, now he's a freezie-pop.
Cartman, Stan and Kyle are on their knees in the snow.
AN - pan over to Cartman
54
120
SOUTH PARK
* "434" is Cut
PAGE 175
432
433
433 cont.
Now we see that Kenny is standing in front of the boys, frozen like Jack Nicholson in The Shining.
STAN
(Dude) do you think if we hit him with a shovel he'd shatter?
KYLE
I dunno, let's find out.
Make Sure head is high enough so we dont have layering problem w/ mouth & jacket.
36
121

Just then, Mephesto blinks his eyes open.

MEPHESTO
Where... Where am I?

CHEF
You're at the hospital, Mr. Mephesto. You were shot.
Now we don't know who tried to shoot you, but -

MEPHESTO
Oh, I'm sure it was my brother again.
He tries to shoot me every month.

CHEF
Oh.

DOCTOR
Where is the little fat boy?
He'll be delighted that Mephesto is awake.

CHEF
He went off looking for Kenny.

EXT. HOSPITAL - DAY

Cartman, Stan and Kyle are on their knees in the snow.

STAN
He was a good friend, and I'll miss him.

KYLE
He was very brave... He risked his life
so that Mephesto could live.

CARTMAN
Yeah, and now he's a freezie-pop.

Now we see that Kenny is standing in front of the boys, frozen like Jack Nicholson in 'The Shining'.

STAN
Dude, do you think if we hit him
with a shovel he'd shatter?

KYLE
I dunno, let's find out.

EXT. 'AMERICA'S MOST WANTED' HEADQUARTERS

A shovel appears through the snow. Jimbo squeezes his way out and takes a deep breath of the crisp morning air. One by one, the townspeople all step out of the building and look up at the warm sun.

MR. GARRISON
Oh, it's over... We're free!

OFFICER BARBRADY
Yes. But at what cost, Mr. Garrison? At what cost?

A guilty hush falls over everyone.

JIMBO
Listen everybody, we did what we had to in there.

MAYOR
But... How will we live with ourselves now?

NED
One day at a time, Mayor... One day at a time.

The camera PULLS BACK up and over the snow-capped mountains as Erin Neville sings 'Ave Maria'.

ERIN NEVILLE
'Aaaa... Ve Mariiiiii-aaaaa...'

MR. GARRISON
Well, I'm bringing home some Eric Roberts in a doggie bag, does anybody else want some?

FADE OUT.

EPILOGUE

INT. HELL'S PASS HOSPITAL - DAY

Everyone is gathered in Mephesto's room much like they were in the very first scene.

MEPHESTO
I'm glad you all could come... I can finally reveal who the father of Eric Cartman is... But first, I want to thank Kenny McCormick for sacrificing his life...

CARTMAN
JUST TELL US ALREADY!!!

MEPHESTO
Alright, alright, alright. The father of Eric Cartman is... Say did anybody see that 'Terrance and Phillip' special last month? Wasn't that just the funniest thing ever?

CARTMAN
Goddammit! Tell me who my father is!

Everyone looks around nervously.

MEPHESTO (cont'd)
Alright, as I said before, the father is somebody in this room... The father is -

Cartman's eyes grow wide.

MEPHESTO
MS. CARTMAN!!!!

HUGE STING - Everybody gasps, then looks confused.

CHEF
What?!

MS. CARTMAN
Yes... It's true.

MR. GARRISON
No, that doesn't make sense.

MEPHESTO
Yes, it took quite a while for me to understand as well. You see, Mrs. Cartman is a hermaphrodite.

MR. GARRISON
Meaning what?

MEPHESTO
Meaning that she has both male and female genitals.

MS. CARTMAN
It's true.

Everybody looks sick. Cartman's head is reeling.

CHEF
You mean that at the drunken barn dance... When we all got together with her, she was a HE?

MEPHESTO
No, no, not exactly, but she did have a penis.

Everybody in the room throws up.

MEPHESTO
The fact of the matter is, hermaphrodites cannot bear children, so Ms. Cartman's DNA match with Eric can only mean that SHE is his father. And she got another woman pregnant at the drunken barn dance.

CARTMAN
Oh man this is fuckin' weak!!

STAN
DUDE, you're a big fat ass,
AND your mom's a hermaphlight!!

MS. CARTMAN
I'm sorry I never told you, Eric. I just thought maybe it would be a little shocking to you.

CARTMAN
(Sarcastic)
Oh wow, gee whizz you think so, Ma?!

MEPHESTO
Well, that's that. Thank you all for playing.

Everybody starts walking away, dazed.

CARTMAN
No, No! Wait a minute! If she's my dad, then who's my mom?

Pause...

NARRATOR
Who is Eric Cartman's mother? Is it - Ms. Crabtree? Sheila Broslovski? The Mayor?

CARTMAN
OH FORGET IT!!

FIN